[BY AUTHORITY.]

A NEW SYSTEM

OF

SWORD EXERCISE,

WITH A

MANUAL OF THE SWORD FOR OFFICERS,

MOUNTED AND DISMOUNTED;

FORMS TO BE OBSERVED ON INSPECTIONS, REVIEWS, PARADES, ETC., ETC.

By MATTHEW J. O'ROURKE,

LATE CAPTAIN U. S. VOLUNTEERS; AUTHOR OF "SWORD EXERCISE ILLUSTRATED," "A TREATISE ON SWORDS AND SWORDSMANSHIP, ANCIENT AND MODERN," ETC.

The Naval & Military Press Ltd

Published by

The Naval & Military Press Ltd
Unit 5 Riverside, Brambleside
Bellbrook Industrial Estate
Uckfield, East Sussex
TN22 1QQ England

Tel: +44 (0)1825 749494

www.naval-military-press.com
www.nmarchive.com

*In reprinting in facsimile from the original, any imperfections are inevitably reproduced
and the quality may fall short of modern type and cartographic standards.*

General Orders, }   WAR DEPARTMENT,
No. 27.   ADJUTANT GENERAL'S OFFICE,
                      Washington City, May 21, 1872.

The following Order, received from the War Department the 10th instant, is published for the information and guidance of the Army:—

Order in regard to a System of Sword Exercise:

The Board of Officers for the revision of the Army Regulations, having examined the System of Sword Exercise prepared by Captain MATTHEW J. O'ROURKE, and recommended its adoption, it is selected for the use and instruction of the officers of the Army of the United States, and will be duly regarded by them.

                BY ORDER OF THE SECRETARY OF WAR,
                           E. D. TOWNSEND,
                                 Adjutant-General.

Official:

      J. P. MARTIN,
                      Assistant Adjutant-General.

Entered, according to Act of Congress, in the year 1872, by MATTHEW J. O'ROURKE, in the office of the Librarian of Congress, at Washington.

BRADSTREET PRESS.

PREFACE.

It must be obvious to every man with the instincts of a soldier, that uniformity in the manual of the sword is as indispensable among officers as proficiency in the manual of the musket among the men. It must be equally obvious that, so long as the sword is the recognized weapon for officers, self-respect and the requirements of the service demand that they should be thoroughly familiar with its uses.

Seven years have elapsed since the first edition of this work was published. It was prepared, under many disadvantages, during the war, and was necessarily crude and imperfect. It contained the germs of an improved system, however; and, immediately on its issue from the press, was submitted to the inspection of many of the most distinguished officers in the service. With the generous appreciation of brave men, they hailed it as an improvement on any similar work that had previously been published, and recommended its adoption for the use of the army.

Several new illustrations, besides additional text, have been added to the present edition. These are nearly all copied from photographs, and represent with tolerable accuracy the several positions they are intended to illustrate; while a front and a profile view of the most important positions is given on the same page—thus obviating the necessity of turning over a number of pages to find illustrations that are frequently referred to in the text.

When I have deemed it necessary to differ from other authors, and to point out what appear to be inaccuracies or inconsistencies in their works, I have not done so in any spirit of self-adulation, nor from any desire to depreciate what they have done, but simply for the purpose of correcting what I believe to be errors.

I have not introduced any innovation through mere caprice or to gratify any personal feeling. My sole aim has been to present a simple, consistent, practicable system, from which officers may derive some useful information. Should the work be found either interesting or instructive by those for whom it is intended, my object in preparing it will have been attained.

New York, *May*, 1872.

CONTENTS.

	PAGE
Introductory	7

THE MANUAL—DISMOUNTED.

Draw Swords	14
The Salute at a Halt	18
The Salute on the March	21
Return Swords	24
Dress Parade	26
Reviews	28
Rules to be Observed by Staff Officers	29
Instructions for Non-Commissioned Staff Officers	30
Inspections	30
Funeral Ceremonies	31
How to Rest the Sword-Arm	31
How the Sword may be Worn	32
Double Time	33

THE MANUAL—MOUNTED.

Draw Swords	34
The Salute	38
Return Swords	41
Sword, Description of	42

CONTENTS.

SWORD EXERCISE.

	PAGE
The Positions	43
The Cuts	48
The Guards	55
Cuts and Guards Combined	65
Attack and Defence	67
Observations on Different Methods of Cutting	88
Points and Parries	91
Observations on Thrusting	92
Feints	107
Independent Practice	110
Opposing the Small-sword	116
Opposing the Bayonet	116
General Observations	118

INTRODUCTORY.

Those who desire to become familiar with the use of their swords will find sufficient in the following pages to form a fair basis upon which to commence, but the degree of proficiency they may attain must rest entirely with themselves.

Some gentlemen may find it convenient to say that no opportunity occurs when an officer can use his sword; apparently unmindful of the fact that an officer who is unacquainted with the use of his sword will not be disposed to seek such an opportunity, and that, if the opportunity did occur, he would be unable to defend himself. Others may say that the improvements that have been made in fire-arms preclude the possibility of getting sufficiently close to an enemy to engage in a hand-to-hand encounter; forgetting that the application of gunpowder to war purposes inspired a terror in the soldiers of the fourteenth century such as no improved fire-arms can ever inspire in soldiers of the present day. The wildest and most irrational stories were circulated in reference to it, and the most diabolical powers attributed to it; but in the early wars between Russia and Turkey, fire-arms had no terrors for the Turks, who, armed with scimitars, compelled the best troops in the Russian Empire to seek shelter behind *chevaux-de-frise* to escape their terrible blades.

Nor was it merely the Bashi-bazouks, Circassians, Mamelukes, Sikhs, and other wild tribes that evinced this contempt for fire-arms. Gustavus Adolphus and Charles XII led their cavalry over everything that opposed them, annihilating whole regiments of infantry, and cutting down the artillerists at their guns. So, too, with Seydlitz and Ziethen, who upset the pet theories of all the old officers of the Prussian army, and revolutionized the military systems of Europe.

Later, the magnificent Murat dazzled the world with the brilliancy of his achievements; while Junot, Kellerman, Caulincourt, Milhaud, Dallas, Uxbridge, Ponsonby, Somerset, and Scarlett, have performed such prodigies of valor as will cause their names to be handed down to posterity so long as the human race is capable of appreciating brave men.

But, it may be said that these were cavalry officers, and that their success was due to the concerted and well-directed action of their troops, rather than to their personal bravery or proficiency in the use of arms. Nothing could be more remote from the truth. If Murat had not been a superb swordsman he could not have led his men as he did, nor could he have inspired them with that confidence which was so essential to success. Distinct from this, history is filled with instances where distinguished officers have had to defend their lives with their swords, and where the personal bravery of a single man has often exercised the most extraordinary influence on the fate of nations.

When only twenty years of age, Cæsar saved the life of a Roman soldier in battle, by interposing himself between his wounded comrade and his assailant, and received the civic crown from his general. The personal daring of T. Manlius, in accepting the challenge of a gigantic Gaul, and defeating him in the presence of the armies of Rome and Gaul, so demoralized the invaders that they were defeated in the next battle, and the fate of Rome was, for the time, averted.

Dauntless bravery, and a thorough mastery of his arms, raised Sparticus from the position of a slave to be the leader of a formidable army that shook Rome to its foundation. The magnificent courage of Richard Cœur de Lion, and Godfrey of Bouillon, won admiration from friend and foe alike; while the Chevalier Bayard will long be regarded as the model for knightly soldiers of every age and clime.

The personal bravery of officers has often enabled them to snatch victory from defeat, and to save their troops from utter annihilation. This has rarely been more strikingly illustrated than in the case of Mortier, at the battle of Diernstein. Hemmed in between overwhelming numbers of the enemy, the fate of his army seemed inevitable; but his own heroic courage, and the terrible effect with which he swept his sword in rapid circles about him, roused his men to almost superhuman efforts, and enabled him to triumph over impending disaster.

At the battle of Neuwied, Ney, when unhorsed, and thrown to the ground, was attacked by six dragoons; but he sprang to his feet and laid about him so furiously with his sword, that they were unable to capture him until an additional force came to their aid, and not even then until after his sword had broken off short in his hand. Early in his military career, Ney did not hesitate to meet a sword-master in combat; and when he enjoyed the title of "bravest of the brave," and the rank of a Marshal of France, he did not shrink from leading his men into action, nor from crossing swords with any enemy who opposed him. And Augereau, who was scarcely inferior in personal daring to Ney, when titles and honors had been showered upon him, and he had won the greatest boon that can be conferred upon a French soldier—the marshal's baton—was wont to refer with pride to his early achievements as a fencing-master.

Had Lannes been less brave or less familiar with the use of his sword, the bridge of Lodi might not have been carried. Or, at Waterloo, if the sword of Uxbridge had not taken off the uplifted arm of the Frenchman who was battering down the door of the farm-house of La Haye Sainte, the fate of the day might have been different.

These, and a thousand other names and incidents of similar import, recur to the mind as we glance back through the dim vista of years, and look, in imagination, at the great battle-fields of the world. The most brilliant soldiers that the world has yet produced recognized the importance of knowing how to use their weapons; and they recognized the equally important fact that, if an officer fails to acquit himself properly, it is of little consequence whether his failure arises from apathy or incompetence.

Bravery is not the peculiar attribute of any particular nation or race. The tendency of all armies after the close of a war in which they have been successful is to retrograde. The Prussians, under Frederick the Great, defied the combined power of France, Austria and Russia, but were shattered to pieces by one of these powers at Jena; and the troops that had been victorious at Jena were crushed and routed at Waterloo. Again, the French triumphed over the Austrians in Italy, and in turn they were literally overwhelmed at Sedan.

No intelligent man will pretend that these results are to be attributed to any change in the physical courage of the men composing these several armies. The cause must be traced to the improvements, or absence of improvement, in the systems under which they operated, and the difference in the energy and efficiency of the officers commanding them.

A NEW SYSTEM

OF

SWORD EXERCISE.

THE MANUAL OF THE SWORD—DISMOUNTED.

Officers will invariably draw their swords without waiting for any order, before assuming command of troops. If the scabbard be hooked up, it should be unhooked before the sword is drawn, and every motion in the manual should be executed with the same precision that would be expected from the men in the manual of arms. The motions having been completed and the sword being at a "carry," the scabbard will, if an officer is on foot, be invariably hooked up; if mounted, the scabbard will be allowed to hang at the full extent of the straps.

When a class is to be instructed, the following rules will be observed:

The class being formed in single rank, at intervals of one pace, swords in scabbards, suspended at the

14   DRAW SWORDS.

full extent of the straps, the instructor will command:

Slow time—DRAW SWORDS.

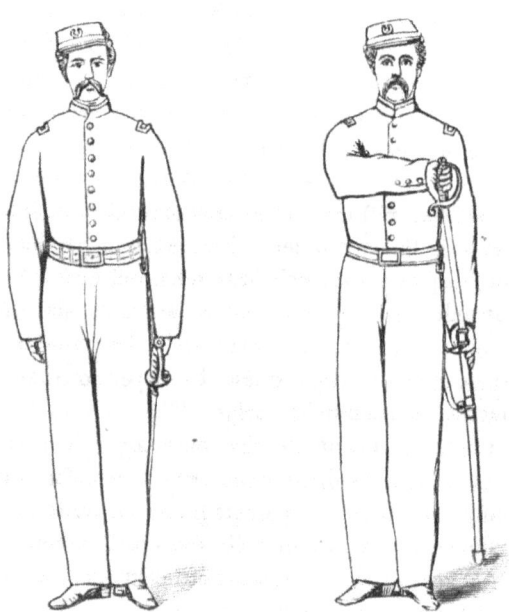

First Motion.

First motion:—Take the scabbard loosely in the left hand, just below the upper ring; raise the sword up slightly, so that the right hand can reach the grip without bending the body; bring the right hand across the body and seize the grip between the thumb and fingers, with a light, easy pressure; turn the edge of the sword round to the left and rear, and, at the same time, raise the right hand, thumb underneath and back inwards, until it is opposite the left nipple; left arm straight, and hand holding the scabbard.

Second motion:—At the command "two," raise the right hand, back inwards, until it is in front of, and six inches from, the face; as soon as the point of the blade has cleared the scabbard, turn the hand quickly and lower it until the top of the thumb comes a little below the chin; the sword nearly perpendicular, edge to the left, and thumb extended along the back of the grip.

Third motion:—At the command "three," lower the hand to its natural position by the side, with the back of the sword resting against the hollow of the shoulder. On completing the third motion, take the upper ring of the scabbard between the thumb and first finger of the left hand; raise the hand until the tips of the fingers touch the lower curve

DRAW SWORDS.

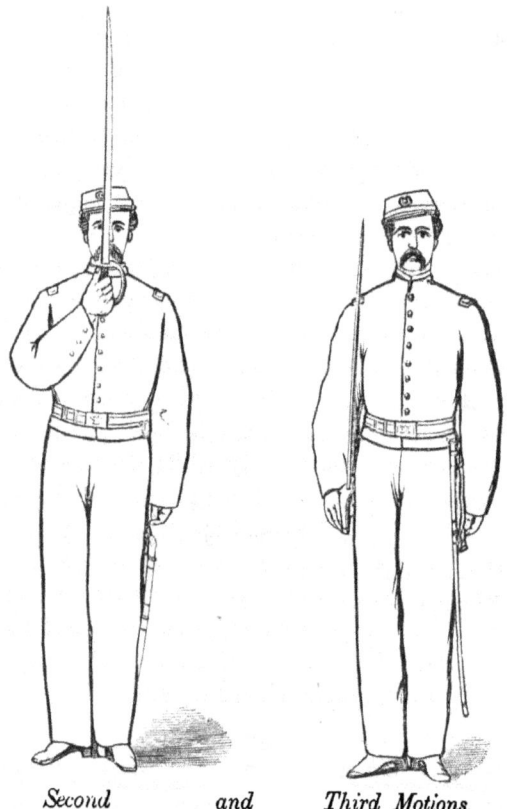

Second and *Third Motions.*

of the hook attached to the waist-belt; slip the ring over the hook, and let the hand fall naturally by the side.

DRAW SWORDS.

The object of turning the sword around, so that the edge is up, in drawing and returning, is twofold: It protects both the edge of the sword and the bell of the scabbard; while, in returning, the curve of the blade will cause it to glide home to the hilt without any necessity for carrying the hand down—a movement that has the appearance of being stiff and constrained.

On coming to a carry, the arms should be allowed to hang naturally by the sides, without any contraction of the muscles; the sword should be held between the first two fingers and thumb—nearly the same as a pen; and if the grip is short, and the guard much curved, it should be held between the first finger and thumb only, while the tips of the remaining fingers should be placed outside, and under the pommel. Should the instructor perceive that any member of the class finds it difficult to extend his arm, he will take the sword from him and cause him to stand to "attention," and then place the sword between his thumb and fingers, without allowing him to bend his arm.

THE SALUTE—AT A HALT.

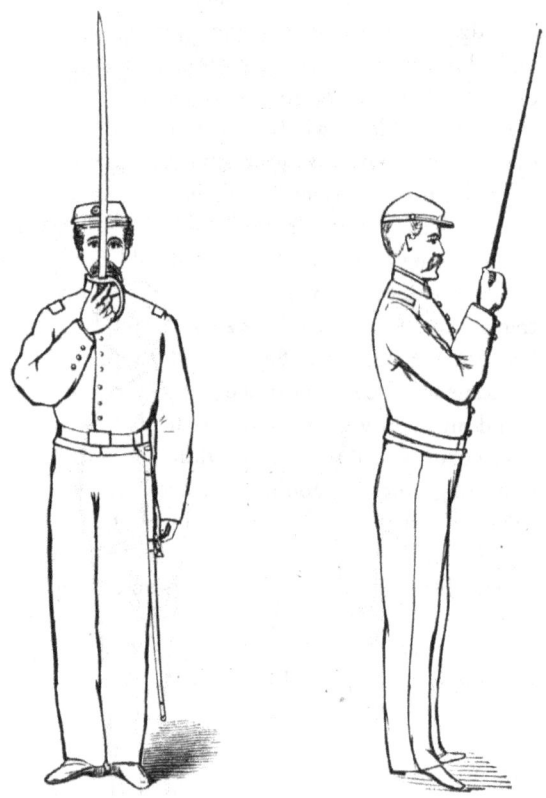

THE SALUTE—AT A HALT.

First motion :—Raise the right hand until it comes

THE SALUTE—AT A HALT. 19

a little below, and about six inches in front of, the chin; edge of the sword to the left, point inclining to the front; thumb extended along the back of the grip, and the nails towards the face.

This position is called the "Recover."

Second motion:—Lower the hand to the full extent

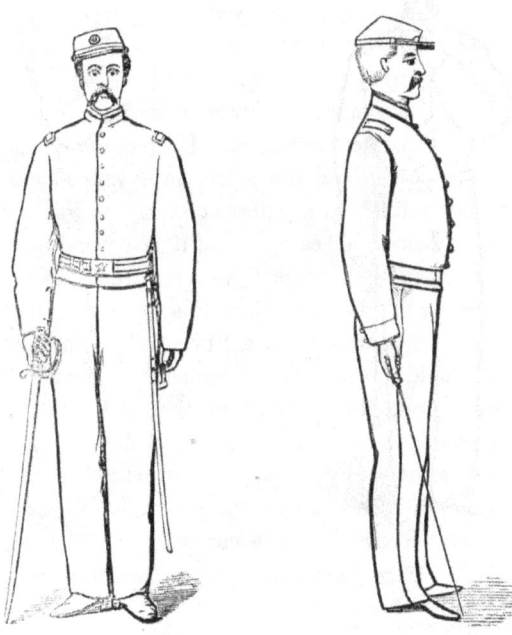

of the arm (if the length of the blade will permit), edge of the sword to the left, point to the right-front, elbows close to the sides, and the blade the prolongation of the arm.

The moment the sword has been brought down to the position just described, the salute is completed, just the same as the "present" is completed the moment the musket is brought to the prescribed position in front of the centre of the body; and, with the sword as with the musket, to come back to the position from which either movement is executed, involves a separate command and a separate movement. If troops were at an "order arms," and the officer in command desired to bring them to a "present arms," he would first bring them to a "carry;" and if he desired to bring them from the "present" to the "order," he would do so by first bringing them to a "carry." In other words, in coming from a "present" to an "order" he would reverse the movements by which they came from the "order" to the "present." The same rule must apply to the sword in coming from the "salute" to the "carry." In coming from the "carry" to the "salute" the sword is first brought to the "recover," and in coming from the "salute" to the "carry" the sword must pass, by inversion, over the same space.

Carry Swords.

First motion:—Bring the sword to the "recover," with the edge to the left, and the hand in the same position as described in the second motion of drawing swords.

Second motion:—Lower the hand to its natural position by the side, with the back of the sword resting against the hollow of the shoulder.

The Salute on the March.

When troops pass in review, in either common or quick time, officers will invariably salute the reviewing officer the first time they pass; but should they pass more than once, they will not salute. If, for any reason, the troops should be required to pass in double time, and they have not previously passed in common or quick time, mounted officers only will salute. The rule to be observed in regard to the manner of making the salute is as follows:

When within six paces of the reviewing officer, bring the sword to the "recover," advancing the right hand for that purpose, at the same moment and in the same time that the left foot is advanced; allow the hand to remain in that position until the left foot is again advanced, and bring the sword and foot down at the same moment; at the same time the head should be turned slightly to the right, so as to look at the officer who is being saluted.

If an officer will take a dozen paces, allowing the arms to move naturally by his side, he will find that the right hand will move forward at the same moment that the left foot is brought to the front; and if, in passing the reviewing officer, he attempts to raise his sword when his right foot is being advanced, it will check the natural motion of the left hand and produce a jar, and a stiff, constrained movement of the whole person—hence the necessity for observing the rule that is here laid down. But there is another reason for counting the paces as described. If the salute is made in this manner, the time occupied in making it must correspond with the time in which the troops are moving, and must be the same for all officers moving at the same rate of speed.

After the sword has been brought down to the "salute," it will remain in that position until six paces have been made, when the motions in the "carry" will be commenced. In these motions the same time will be observed; the sword will be brought to the "recover" as the left foot touches the ground, and will remain in that position for one pace; on the left foot again coming to the ground, the sword will be brought to the "carry."

If a class is to be instructed in the salute on the march, it will be done in the following manner:

The instructor will form the class in single rank,

one pace apart, with swords at a carry, and will explain the object of the drill. He will then command:

Three paces to the front—MARCH.

The class will immediately step off with the left foot, bringing the sword to the "recover" at the same moment, keeping it there for one pace, and bringing it down to the "salute" simultaneously with the completion of the third pace. On coming to a "carry," the instructor will use the same command, and the class will execute the first motion as they make the first pace, and complete the movement as the heels are brought together on the third pace. Having practiced the class sufficiently in this way, to enable them to understand the principle involved, and to count the time correctly, the instructor will cause the "salute" and the "carry" to be executed in *eleven paces*, without halting until the eleven paces have been completed. To do this he will place himself in front of the centre of the class, and distant from it sufficiently to enable him to have the entire class under his eyes; he will then command:

Eleven paces to the front—MARCH.

As the class steps off, the instructor will commence to step back, bringing his sword to the "recover" with the first pace, and making each motion simultaneously with the class, bringing the

RETURN SWORDS.

sword to the "recover" with the ninth pace, and to a "carry" on the completion of the eleventh pace.

RETURN SWORDS.

First motion :—Take the scabbard in the left hand,

RETURN SWORDS. 25

just below the upper ring, and raise it until the ring has cleared the hook; extend the left arm to its full length, and turn the hand outwards, so as to bring the edge of the scabbard up, with the bell inclining slightly to the front; at the same time bring the sword to the recover, and remain steady.

Second motion:—Keep an easy hold of the grip, and allow the point of the sword to fall over to the left-and-rear, *with the edge up;* insert the point of

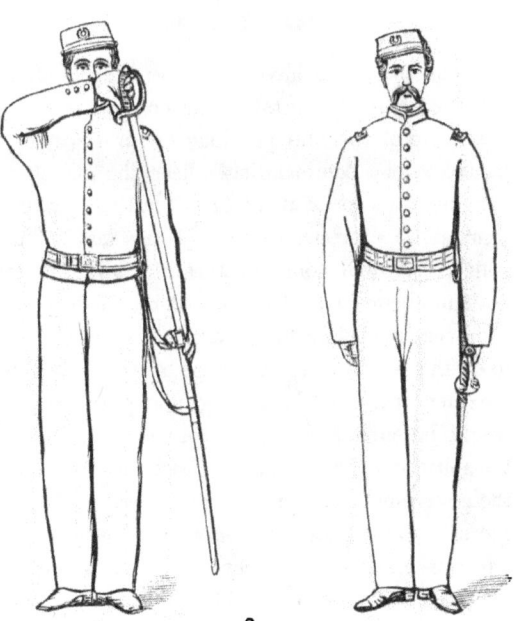

the sword in the scabbard, and lower the hand about six inches.

Third motion:—With a quick, muscular movement of the fingers and thumb, send the sword to the hilt in the scabbard, without lowering the hand below the left nipple, and the next moment allow the scabbard to slip easily from the left hand, and resume the position of "attention."

Dress Parade.

When the ranks have been opened and aligned, and the adjutant has taken his position in front of the centre of the line, previous to turning over the parade to the commanding officer, the officers will remain with swords at a "carry" until the adjutant commands: "present arms," at the last sound of which, they will come to a salute. Officers must not anticipate an order, nor commence to execute a movement, before the command has been given; to do this would be to encourage unsteadiness among the men, particularly among young soldiers, and would be subversive of discipline, and opposed to the spirit and the letter of the laws that are made for the government of the military forces. They will, therefore, wait until the command, "present arms," has been given, before they move, and will observe the same rule in coming back to a "carry"—waiting until the command has been finished, and going through the motion with the most scrupulous precision.

On facing about, to announce that the parade is formed, the adjutant will salute the commanding officer, and will remain in that position until directed to take his post, when he will bring his sword to a "carry." At the command: "carry arms," the officers will bring their swords to a "carry," *and will remain in that position*, unless the command "parade rest," is given, when they will drop the point of the sword between the feet, edge to the right, palm of the right hand resting on the pommel, and palm of left hand resting on the back of the right. In exercising the troops in the manual of arms, the commanding officer can repeat the commands: "carry arms," "present arms," "port arms," "charge bayonets," "order arms," etc., etc., as often as he thinks proper, but these commands are not intended to apply to the officers, who at best could only comply with a portion of them; hence, they should remain steady at the "carry."

The adjutant having received the reports, read the orders, reported, and being directed by the commanding officer to dismiss the parade, will face the line and command:

"*Parade is Dismissed.*"

He will then return his sword, and, at the same time, all the other officers will return their swords—*taking the time from the adjutant.*

In drawing and returning swords, commanding officers will conform to the rule laid down in the manual of the sword for officers on foot.

REVIEWS.

The rule that requires officers to salute only once at dress parade, does not apply to a review. Here they will salute when the men present arms at the commencement of the review, and *once* in passing the reviewing officer, in the manner described under the head of the "salute on the march," and again, when the troops present arms at the conclusion of the review.

If the troops pass in "*Double Time,*" not having previously passed in quick time, mounted officers will salute the reviewing officer in the usual manner, but officers on foot will conform to the rule laid down under the head "Double Time," and will not salute the reviewing officer. Should they pass in double time after passing in quick time, neither mounted nor dismounted officers will salute.

Rules to be Observed by Staff Officers.

In passing the reviewing officer, the position of staff officers (except adjutants) will be five paces in

PARADES OF CEREMONY. 29

rear of their respective commanding officers. They will have their swords drawn, and will salute the reviewing officer when passing; but *will not* commence the salute* until they have reached the point at which their commanding officer commenced his salute, and will not bring their swords to the "recover" until they have reached the point at which he brought his sword to the "recover."

When staff officers or others, with their swords drawn, approach a superior officer for the purpose of reporting or conveying orders, they will halt when within two or three paces of the officer approached, and salute, remaining at the salute until it has been acknowledged; when, if there be no further occasion for delay, they will bring their swords to a "carry" and proceed to their posts.

---

* In the Appendices to Upton's Tactics (pp. 350–367), it is laid down that all officers shall salute the reviewing officer when *within six paces* of him, and recover their swords when *six paces past him;* while, at page 368 (Appendix II), it is prescribed that staff officers shall salute the reviewing officer "at the *very instant their commanding officers do*, and bring their swords up when they do."

This is an obvious mistake. It is manifest that staff officers cannot conform to the second rule without violating the first. If a general officer or a colonel commences his salute when within six paces of the reviewing officer, and his staff commence the salute at the same moment, the latter will be *eleven paces* from the reviewing officer instead of six; and if a general or a colonel bring his sword to the "recover" when six paces past the reviewing officer, and his staff bring their swords to the recover at the same instant, the latter will have passed the reviewing officer only *one pace*, instead of six, and will not have conformed to the rule previously laid down.

PARADES OF CEREMONY.

Instruction for Non-commissioned Staff Officers.

Non-commissioned staff officers (except at inspection) will keep their swords in the scabbards, and, when passing in review, will salute the reviewing officer with the left hand, in the manner prescribed at page 15 of Upton's Tactics. At inspection they will draw their swords, and, on the approach of the inspecting officer, will bring them to a "recover," with the hand opposite the chin, the sword nearly perpendicular, with the point up.

INSPECTIONS.

When officers take their place at an inspection, they will have their swords drawn and at a "carry," but *will not* bring them to a "recover"* on the approach of the inspecting officer.

---

* An erroneous impression appears to prevail among certain officers of the National Guard as to the position in which the sword should be held while the inspecting officer is passing in front of the officers at inspection. These officers contend that, because the rule is laid down that the inspector is required to inspect "the dress and general appearance of the field and commissioned staff *under arms*," and to pass down the open column, "looking at every rank in front and rear," the officers must bring their swords to a "recover" and turn them round on the approach of the inspector, in the same manner that enlisted men of the cavalry are required to do when their arms are being inspected by their officer. It is difficult to conceive how such an impression could have originated, as a moment's reflection should have convinced any intelligent person that the adoption of such a rule would not be in consonance with either the courtesies or requirements of the service.

Funeral Ceremonies.

When the command is given to a funeral escort to reverse arms, the officers will pass their swords under the right arm, bending the arm and raising the hand until it is on a level with the elbow, the point of the sword to the rear, the blade nearly horizontal, and the edge up; at the same time they will pass the left hand behind the back and grasp the blade. When the escort "rests on arms," the officers will drop the point of the sword between the feet, edge to the right, right hand on the pommel, palm of left hand resting on the back of the the right, and head slightly bowed. On the escort coming to a "carry arms," preparatory to loading, the officers will come to "attention," and bring their swords to a "carry."

How to Rest the Sword-Arm.

When troops are being exercised, and are kept for a considerable time without coming to a "rest," officers may become fatigued from carrying their swords continuously in the same position. On such occasions, if an officer desires to rest his sword-arm, he will pass the sword diagonally across the body, allowing the back of the blade to rest in the hollow of the left arm, bending that arm at the elbow, and taking the grip and the pommel of the sword in the palm of the left hand, while he allows the right hand to fall naturally by his side. Care should be taken to avoid the practice of dropping the point of the sword, or swinging it about like a walking-stick or an umbrella.

How the Sword may be Worn.

Paragraph 1,521 of the Army Regulations provides as follows:

"When on foot, the *sabre* will be suspended from the hook attached to the belt."

Many officers interpret this so as to make it apply to themselves, and think they are required to keep their swords hooked up. This is a mistake. The rule is intended to apply to enlisted men of the cavalry and artillery, and is meant to secure uniformity amongst troops of these arms of the service, when dismounted; but has no reference to officers of any branch of the army.

In going to and returning from parades, drills, &c., and when not actually with troops, officers may wear their swords either suspended from the hook attached to the waist-belt or hanging at the full extent of the straps. Or, if they prefer it, they can carry them over the left fore-arm, through the angle formed by bending the arm at the elbow, with the hilt in rear and pressing lightly against the arm and the left side—with the point inclining downwards. This rule applies also to officers visiting sentinels, inspecting quarters, on the route, and on all other occasions when acting individually, and separate from troops, but ceases to apply the moment an officer takes his position at any parade or inspection.

Double Time.*

Whenever it is necessary for an officer to move in double time, he will raise his right hand until it is on a level with the elbow, and carry it to the front, allowing the back of the sword to rest on the shoulder; at the same time he will unhook his scabbard, let it slip forward through his hand until he can grasp it near the centre, allowing it to rest horizontally in the hand, with the arm extended by the side; but, on resuming quick time or coming to a halt, the sword must be immediately brought to a "carry," and the scabbard hooked up.

---

* In the volunteer service several different modes of carrying the sword, when moving in double time, were adopted by the officers of different regiments. Some held the blade at an angle of about forty-five degrees, with the point down, and were liable, should they slip, or strike against any obstruction, to run their sword into any one who happened to be in front of them. Others placed the sword under the left arm, with the point to the rear, and were liable, should they fall, to transfix any one who might be close behind them on the point of their blade. Others, again, passed the sword diagonally across the body, with the point in front of the left shoulder; should they stumble, their hands would naturally be thrown forward to protect them in falling, and the sword would be liable to come in contact with some one in their vicinity.

By following the rule laid down in this system, it will be impossible for an officer to injure either himself or any other person.

The Manual—Mounted.

If a field or staff officer has his sword hooked up, he will invariably unhook it before mounting, and will allow the sword, and the scabbard, when the sword has been drawn, to hang at the full extent of the straps.

In drawing swords, pass the right hand over the bridle-arm and seize the grip with an easy pressure, the fingers encircling the lower part of it, and the thumb extending along the back; at the same time, raise the hand and turn it round so that the edge of the sword shall be directed to the left-and-rear, and the back of the hand opposite the left nipple.

Second motion:—Extend the arm until the back of the hand is in front of the face and the point of the sword has cleared the scabbard; then turn the hand quickly, bringing the point of the sword round close to the left shoulder, and check it when it has attained a perpendicular position, with the point up and the edge to the left; lower the hand until the top of the thumb (which should be extended along the back of the grip) comes in front of, and about six inches from, the chin.

THE MANUAL—MOUNTED.

DRAW SWORDS.

Third motion:—Lower the hand to an easy, natural position by the side, and, in doing so, allow the thumb to slip from the back to the side of the grip, and the fingers to the opposite side, both pointing in the direction of the pommel of the sword, and encircling the grip, nearly the same as the thumb and fingers encircle a pen. The arm should be slightly bent, and the elbow carried to the rear, and not off to the right, while the first joint of the thumb and the tip of the first finger should rest against the outside of the thigh.

THE CARRY.

The Salute—Mounted.

The salute, at a halt or on the march, will be executed in the manner prescribed for officers on foot; the time should be counted, and each motion should be made with deliberation and precision.

In passing the reviewing officer, mounted officers should not turn out abruptly. They are only required to pass in review before officers superior in rank to themselves, and to hurry through with the parade, or to slur over any movement themselves, would be, at least, discourteous to a superior officer.

THE SALUTE.

THE MANUAL—MOUNTED.

RETURN SWORDS.

THE MANUAL—MOUNTED.

RETURN SWORDS—MOUNTED.

The left hand should not touch the scabbard in returning swords. The sword should be brought to the "recover," with the point up and the edge to the left. Allow the point to fall over the bridle-arm, *with the edge down*, and insert it a few inches in the scabbard; then turn the hand, as in drawing swords, so that the edge of the blade will be directed to the left-and-rear, and with a quick, muscular, movement of the thumb and fingers, send the sword to the hilt in the scabbard, without carrying the hand below the left nipple, and allow the right hand to fall naturally by the side.

SWORDS.

A difference of opinion appears to exist among different authorities as to the proper divisions of a sword; some contending that it should be divided into three parts, and others that it should be divided into two. Without attempting to settle the question, or even to enter on the merits of the dispute, it will answer the present purpose if I say that the half of the sword nearest the hilt is generally called the "Fort," and the half nearest the point, the "Feeble." The edge of the lower part (or fort) of the sword should be blunt, and should be used for guarding, while the edge of the upper half (or feeble) should be sharp and should be used for cutting.

The term hilt, is applied to that part of the sword between the blade and the extreme end of the grip. The term grip or handle, to that part of the hilt that is grasped by the thumb and fingers. The part of the hilt that covers the hand is called the guard, and when it is composed of separate bars of metal they are called branches, and the extreme end of the grip is called the pommel.

Swords are classified under three heads: Small-swords, short-swords and broad-swords; but the generic term "sword" applies to all of them, and for ordinary purposes it is better to employ this term, when speaking of swords, on the same principle that we use the term "arms" in the manual of the musket, regardless of the name by which it would be designated if it were necessary to describe it for a specific purpose.

Cavalry are supposed to be armed with broad-swords; line officers of infantry with short-swords; and general officers and certain staff officers with small-swords.

The Positions.

There are three positions in sword exercise, a knowledge of which should be acquired before any attempt is made to practice with swords. The first position is that in which a man receives all the cuts and thrusts of his opponent; the heels are close together, the feet at right angles, the knees well braced, and the weight of the body thrown mainly on the left leg, so that an instantaneous movement can be made either backward or forward. The second position is that in which a man first crosses swords with his opponent (technically called "engaging"). In this position both knees are bent, and the weight of the body is thrown on the left leg, while the right foot is kept free, ready to move out to the third or back to the first position, as occasion may require. The third position is that in which a man delivers all the cuts and thrusts that are intended to be effective. Here the body is thrown forward at the same instant that the right foot is carried to the front, while the left leg is extended and the weight of the body is transferred to the right leg.

When a class is to be instructed, the following rule will be observed:

The instructor will form the class in single rank, at intervals of one pace, and take his position at a sufficient distance from its front and centre to

44 SWORD EXERCISE.

enable him to see the movements of each person in the class. Having explained the object of the drill and gone through the motions to illustrate the movement, he will command:

First position:—At the last sound of the word

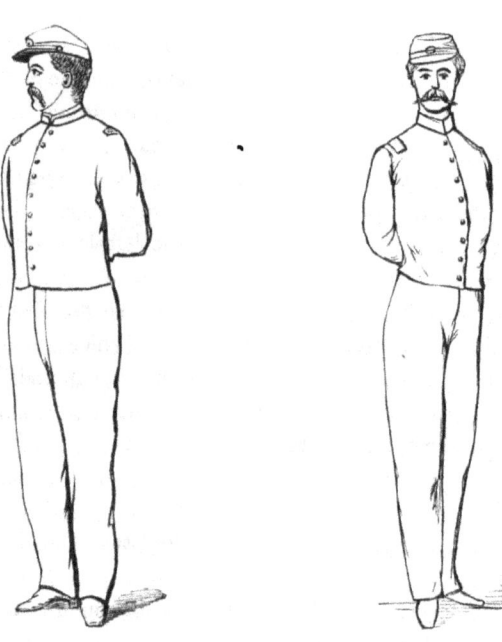

"position," the class will make a half face to the left, carrying the right foot to the left until the heel of that foot presses against the hollow of the left foot; feet at right angles, right foot pointing straight to the front; at the same time raise the hands behind the back until they are on a level with the elbows, the left hand between the back and the right arm, palm outwards; the right hand (palm up) supporting the left arm just below the elbow; the left shoulder carried well to the rear, face full to the front, and the weight of the body on the left leg.

Second position:—Bend both knees, the right to the front, the left to the left, until they are about six inches apart; pause a moment; then raise the right foot sufficiently high to clear the ground, and advance it about 18 inches, straight to the front, keeping both knees well bent, and the weight of the body on the left leg—the right leg easy and flexible, ready to be drawn back to the first position or advanced to the lunge.

"Advancing" and "retiring" should be practiced in this position. At the order "advance," the right foot is raised slightly and advanced about 15 inches; the left foot is then brought up until it is within 15 inches of the right. At the word "retire," the left foot is raised and carried 15 inches to the rear; the right foot is then raised and drawn back to the "second position," and placed on the ground with a quick, sharp beat, called the "single attack," or two beats in quick succession, called the "double attack."

The object of advancing is to gain ground on an

adversary who is disposed to keep out of your reach; and the object of retiring is to keep out of the reach of an impetuous adversary; while the quick beat with the foot is likely to disconcert those who are not in practice.

Third position:—Raise the right foot slightly, and advance it about 18 inches farther to the front; the left foot should be kept firm, and the left leg fully extended. Care should be taken not to lunge out too far. The right leg below the knee must be kept perpendicular, and the weight of the body on the ball of the right foot.

These positions should be practised, changing from 1st to 3d, and from 3d to 1st and 2d, until they are understood and can be executed with facility.

Having completed the above movements, the class will buckle on their swords.

If the class be small, the instructor will form it in single rank, at intervals of two paces, with swords unhooked. If it is large, he will form two ranks, the ranks two paces apart, intervals between the files the same as in single rank, and the files of the rear rank opposite the open space between the files of the front rank. He will commence each lesson by causing the class to draw swords, and salute; calling off each motion in slow time, unless the class has been previously instructed in the manual, in which case the movements will be executed in common time.

The Cuts.

Nominally, there are seven cuts; and the target used at drill, to show the direction of the cuts, is divided by seven lines converging at the centre. It is probable that this was done primarily to make the number of cuts correspond to the number of guards. Otherwise it might be said, with quite as much propriety, that there are but three cuts: one from right to left, one from left to right, and one vertically down the centre. Or it might be claimed that there are three hundred cuts, representing 300° of a circle, as the cut may be directed at any point from No. 7 to No. 3 on the right, and from No. 7 to No. 4 on the left. Beginners stand in the first position, with the feet close together, while making the cuts, and carry the hand to the right and left, allowing the sword to continue the sweep after its point has reached the centre of the target. This is never done in actual practice. When two swordsmen engage they each make a half face to the left, in order to present the smallest possible surface of the body to their opponent, and to cover that surface with the sword. When in this position, an imaginary line runs through the centre of the bodies of the two men. This line is called the line of defence, and the right hand should always be kept as near it as possible. Here the hand becomes the pivot around

SWORD EXERCISE. 49

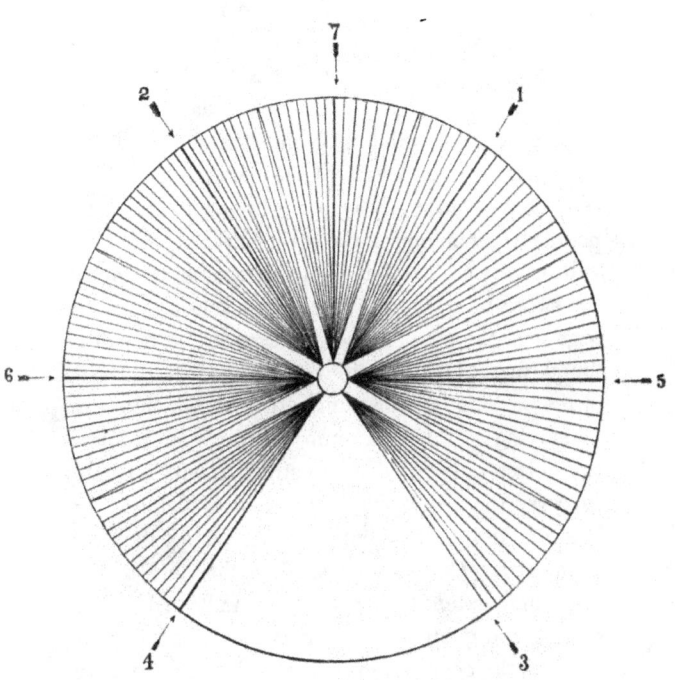

THE CUTS.

which the sword revolves. The first and fourth finger and thumb serve successively as fulcrum and re-acting power on the hilt. The rotatory motion of the sword gives immense velocity to the blade near the point, and engenders a centrifugal force which acts on the body struck. The hand gives the impulse to the sword, but the momentum is increased in the ratio of the length of the blade; hence, if the edge of a sword, midway between the hilt and the point, strikes an object, the effect on the object struck will be very slight; but if, at the moment of impact, the sword be moving at its greatest velocity, and the edge near the point strikes the same body, it will be found that the effect will be increased in the ratio of the increased momentum. If, however, the sword be moving at the maximum velocity, and it misses the object it is intended to strike, it will be liable to carry the hand out of the line of defence, unless the thumb be kept extended along the back of the grip. Care should be taken, therefore, to keep the thumb extended in the manner indicated, in both cutting and guarding; it acts as a lever on the point, changes the centre of gravity at will, counteracts the centrifugal force of the blade, and checks its course instantly when there is occasion to do so.

Preparatory to commencing the cuts, a target, about 36 inches in diameter, should be procured, and placed in a position where it will be opposite the left-centre of the class; the centre of the target breast high. The instructor will place himself close to the target, and will point out the direction of each cut, and will face the target occasionally and go through the motions himself, to illustrate the manner in which the several movements should be executed. By naming the particular part of the person at which the cut is aimed, in connection with the number of the cut, as "Cut one—left cheek," "Cut two—right cheek," &c., the pupil will be able to remember the cuts more readily than he would were they designated by numbers only.

The class being formed in single rank at intervals of two paces, the instructor will commence the lesson by causing the class to draw swords and salute. After coming to a "carry," he will command:

RIGHT, PROVE DISTANCE.

The class (except the right-hand man) will bring the sword to the "recover," pause a moment, turn the head slightly to the right, carry the hand to the right until it is on a level with the shoulder, nails down, the sword pointing to the right and the edge to the rear. The point of the blade must clear the shoulder of the next file to the right of each pupil; and when it is necessary to move, pupils will take ground to the left until they have obtained sufficient distance. This done, the instructor will command:

CARRY SWORDS.

when the swords will be brought to a "carry" without bringing them to the "recover."

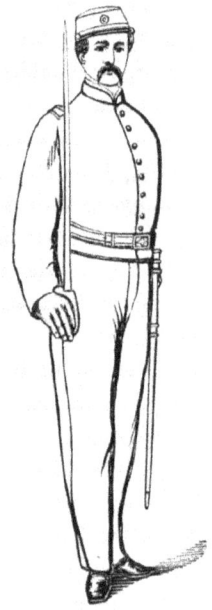

First Position:—The class having brought their swords to a "carry," the instructor will command, "First Position," when the class will make a half face to the left and bring the left hand behind the back.

Assault.

Raise the right hand, arm extended, until it is on a level with the shoulder; carry it a little to the right, and allow the back of the blade, near the point, to rest on the right shoulder, with the edge turned slightly to the right.

Cut One—Left Cheek:—Cut diagonally, with an extended arm, from No. 1 to No. 4, and allow the sword to continue the sweep until it touches the left shoulder; check it there, and extend the arm; hand opposite No. 2, on the target; edge of the sword up, and inclining to the left, with the back of the blade resting on the shoulder.

Cut Two—Right Cheek:—Cut from No. 2 to No. 3; check the sword when it comes in front of the right leg, and turn the edge to the front; point inclining to the rear, with the nails up.

Cut Three—Wrist:—Cut from No. 3 to No. 2; check the sword when the hand comes in front of the left shoulder; allow the point to fall over to the left and rear, with the nails down, the arm extended obliquely across the body, and the hand opposite No. 4.

Cut Four—Leg:—Cut from No. 4 to No. 1; allow the sword to continue the sweep until it touches the right shoulder; edge to the right, arm slightly bent, and nails up.

Cut Five—Left Side:—Extend the arm quickly, and cut, horizontally, from No. 5 to No. 6; turn the nails down when the hand comes opposite No. 6, and allow the sword to continue the sweep until it touches the left shoulder; edge to the left, point to the rear, and the arm slightly bent.

Cut Six—Right Side:—Cut from No. 6 to No. 5, extending the arm the moment the cut is delivered; allow the sword to continue the sweep, and raise the hand until it is above the head; arm slightly bent, point of the sword to the rear (drooping), and the edge up.

Cut Seven—Head:—Cut vertically down from No. 7 to the centre of the target; check the sword and bring it back to the "carry."

The "Cuts" should be repeated several times before the "Guards" are commenced. A lesson should not exceed one hour, and the class should be allowed to "rest" frequently during that time. At the conclusion of each lesson the instructor will cause the class to "return swords" before being dismissed.

SWORD EXERCISE. 55

THE GUARDS.

Guard One—Left Cheek:—Remain in the first position, and carry the sword across to the left, until the hand clears the left shoulder; thumb extended along the back of the grip, edge to the left, and the point well to the front and centre.

SWORD EXERCISE.

Guard Two—Right Cheek:—From the position of "First Guard" the hand is carried across, in front of the body, until it clears the right shoulder; turn the nails to the front, elbow close to the side; edge of the sword to the right, and the point to the front and centre.

SWORD EXERCISE. 57

Guard Three— Wrist:—Lower the hand, and bring it across the body until it comes a little below, and in front of, the left hip; nails up; edge of the sword to the left, with the point in front of the right leg.

Guard Four—Leg:—Turn the hand, nails down, and carry it across until it clears the right hip; edge of the sword to the right, and the point in front of the right leg.

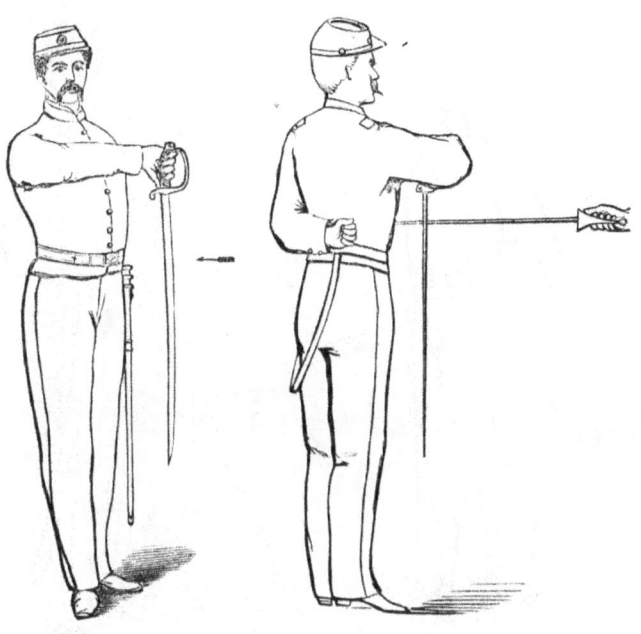

Guard Five—Left Side:—Raise the hand as high as the shoulder, and carry it across to the left; sword perpendicular, six inches from the body point down, and edge to the left.

SWORD EXERCISE.

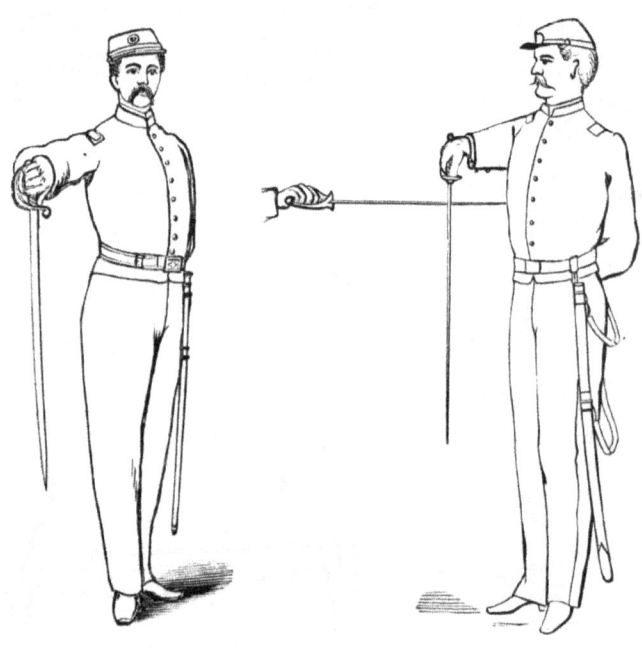

Guard Six—Right Side:— Carry the hand across to the right, until it has cleared the side; the elbow should be pressed well back; the edge of the sword to the right, and the point down.

SWORD EXERCISE.

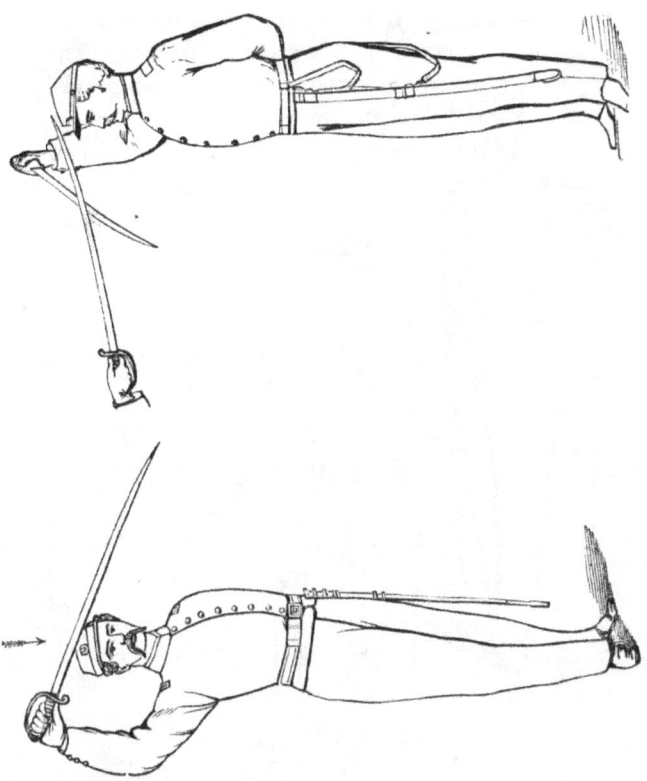

Guard Seven—Head:—Raise the hand above the head, and carry it to the right and front until it clears the right elbow; edge of the sword up, point to the left-front, and on a line with the left shoulder.

SWORD EXERCISE.

The accompanying diagram shows the effect of making the guards in the manner described. The person is entirely surrounded by these seven guards, and no matter what direction the cut may come from, one of the seven guards will be an effectual protection against it.

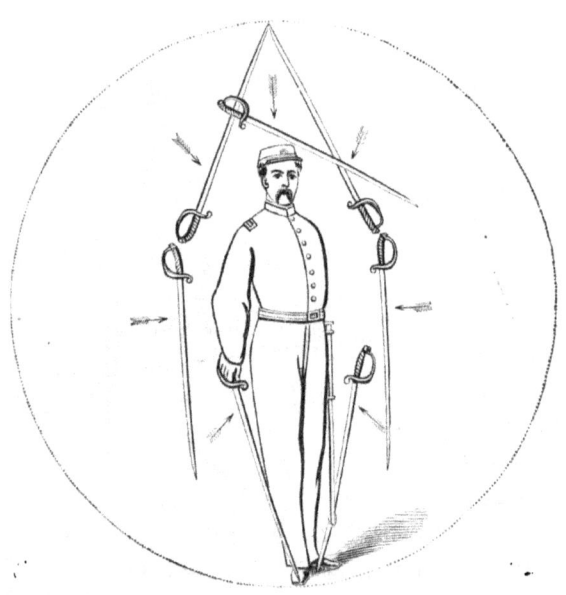

SWORD EXERCISE. 63

As a general rule the guards are made from what is known as the "engaging guard," when the hand is in front of the centre of the body and the sword on the line of defence, already described. To form any of the guards from this position, it is only necessary to move the hand a few inches to the right or left, and to raise or lower the point of the sword according to the direction of the cut. To render a cut effective, the point of the sword must pass over

considerable space, at times describing an arc, and at other times a complete circle. In forming the guards the sword moves on interior lines, forming an acute angle above the head and a similar angle in front of the legs; while the sides are protected by vertical lines on the right and left, and the head and chest are further protected by placing the sword at the angle shown on the diagram, with the point inclining to the front.

For the purpose of familiarizing pupils with the different guards and enabling them to change rapidly from one position to another, the instructor should call the guards off out of their regular order, simply using the commands "head," "leg," "left side," "left cheek," "leg," "head," etc.; and accompanying each command with the corresponding guard.

Celerity of movement is an essential element of success in sword exercise, but there is this important difference to be observed in its application to the cuts and guards: In making a cut, the initial velocity of the sword should be a maximum—the sword being regarded in the light of a projectile; while in guarding, the velocity is increased as the movement progresses, and should attain the maximum the instant before the sword is checked. The necessity for observing these rules will be more apparent as the instruction progresses.

Cuts and Guards Combined.

As soon as the different "Positions," "Cuts," and "Guards" have been sufficiently practised and thoroughly impressed on the mind, they can be "Combined" in the following manner:

Being at the First Position, the command, "Guard," will be given, when the class will immediately step out to the "Second Position," and bring the sword in front of the body; edge to the right, point nearly as high as the eyes, nails down, and the thumb extended along the back of the grip.

This position is known as the "Engaging Guard," and is the one in which a man first crosses swords with his opponent. In this practice there are no sweeping cuts, the sword being invariably checked when it comes opposite the centre of the body, or opposite the centre of the target, if a target be used. The cuts are all delivered in the "Third Position," the head being kept well up and the sword-arm well extended. After delivering each cut, and without waiting for any order, the class will immediately spring up to the "First Position," and form the corresponding guard.

Cut One:—Lunge out to the "Third Position," and deliver the "Cut;" check the sword when it comes in front of the centre of the body; spring back to "First Position," and make the "First Guard."

After making the first guard, the class will remain steady until the instructor has explained the next movement. Having done this, he will command:

Cut Two:—Lunge out to the "Third Position," and deliver the "Cut," checking the sword, as before; spring up to the "First Position," and make the "Second Guard."

Here, it will be perceived, the cut is made by lunging out from the first to the third position, without coming to the intermediate position; and the same rule applies to all the subsequent cuts, until the seven cuts with their corresponding guards have been made. After the seventh guard has been made, the instructor will give the command, "Guard," when the class will spring out to the "Second Position," and bring the sword in front of the centre of the body in the same manner that it is brought previous to delivering the first cut.

Cut Three:—Allow the point of the sword to fall over to the right-and-rear, edge leading, and make the cut with the nails up; check the sword when the hand comes opposite the centre of the body; lower the point, *without turning the hand;* spring back to the "First Position," and make the "Third Guard."

Cut Four:—Turn the hand, throwing the point of the sword over to the left-rear, lunge out, and deliver the cut with the nails down; check the sword in front of the centre of the body; lower the point, *without turning the hand;* spring back with the feet close together, and make the "Fourth Guard."

Cut Five:—Raise the hand as high as the centre of the body; turn it quickly so as to throw the point over to the right; lunge out and cut, breast high, with the nails up. Having delivered the cut, spring back to the "Fifth Guard;" drop the point of the sword; turn the edge to the left, and make the guard.

Cut Six:—Raise the point of the sword and carry it to the rear until the back of the blade nearly touches the left arm; at the same instant lunge out, extend the arm, and cut, breast high, with the nails down; drop the point of the sword, edge to the right; spring up and make the "Sixth Guard."

Cut Seven:—Bring the hand in front of the chest, edge of the sword to the front; sweep the blade round by the left arm, and at the same instant lunge out, raising and extending the arm, and cut vertically down as far as the centre of the body; spring back and make the "Seventh Guard."

Attack and Defence.

As soon as the cuts and guards can be made with precision and rapidity, the class may be practised in the "Attack and Defence." The object of this practice is to familiarize pupils with the mode of cutting at an opponent, and getting back to the guard, to save themselves from the return cut. It serves, also, to give a correct idea of distance, and must inspire pupils with a feeling of security when they find that they can stop a "cut" or turn off a "point" without any difficulty. The cuts should be made lightly: the sword-hand should be always kept as near the centre of the body as possible, and should never be carried far, either to the right or left, for the purpose of making a sweeping cut.

Before commencing this practice, hickory or ash sticks of about 38 inches in length, made in the form of swords, and mounted with sole-leather guards,* should be substituted for the ordinary swords, and the latter should never be used under any circumstance in the attack and defence. The class should be formed in two ranks, facing the instructor, with a distance of two paces between the ranks and two paces between the files of each rank. Being at "attention" (swords at a "carry"), the instructor will command:

Front Rank—About Face:—At this command the

---

* Sole-leather will make an admirable guard. The handle or grip of the stick should be about 6 inches in length, and the leather about 14 inches in length, 3½ inches in width at the widest part, near the blade, and tapering off gradually towards the pommel. An oblong piece, sufficiently long to make room for the blade, should be cut out within about one inch of the wide end, and, after the blade has been passed through the aperture, the small end should be bent over the end of the handle, and fastened down with a screw.

front rank will face about, and if the files do not face each other, the instructor will order one or both ranks to take a side step to the right, and will then command:

First Position:—When both ranks will make a half-face to the left, and bring the left hand behind the back.

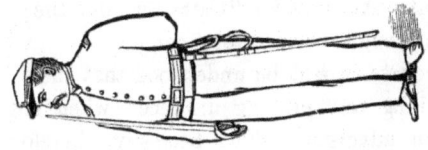

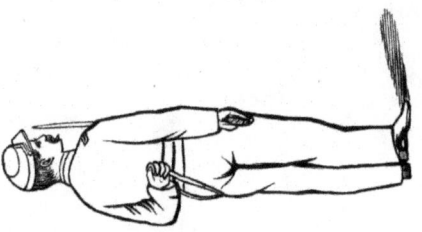

FIRST POSITION.

Front, Prove Distance:—Raise the hand, close in front of the body, and bring the sword to the "Recover;" pause a moment, and extend the arm to the front, edge of the sword to the right, with the thumb extended along the back of the hilt, the point of one sword touching the hilt of the other; the sword of the front rank being above that of the rear rank. At the order, "Carry Swords," the swords will be brought back to the "carry."

Of course it will be understood that there is no such thing as "proving distance" when engaged with an adversary. The necessity, therefore, of marking the distance carefully, must be obvious; and pupils will do well to measure with their eye the exact distance at which they can strike their opponent.

SWORD EXERCISE.

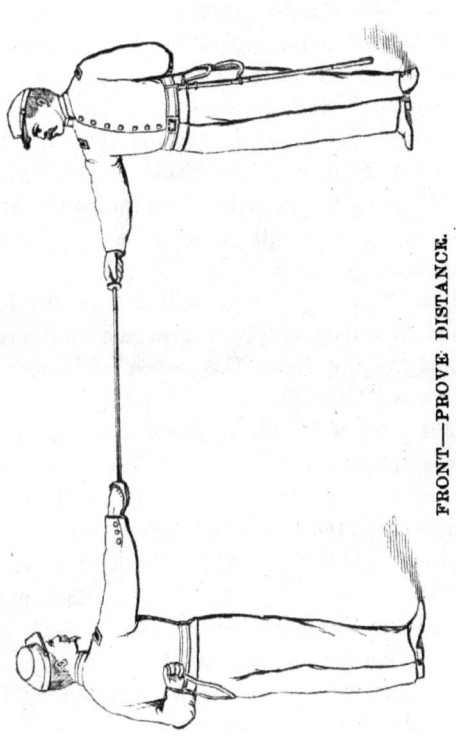

FRONT—PROVE DISTANCE.

Attack and Defence.

Guard:—At the word "Guard," both ranks will step out to the "Second Position," the knees well bent, weight of the body on the left leg, the right hand in front of the centre of the body, the point of the sword nearly as high as the eyes, and the edge to the right, with the blades crossed (edges touching) about twelve inches from the point; hold the sword steady, with a slight, even pressure against your opponent's blade.

Ordinarily the front rank will deliver the first cut, and the instructor will give the cautionary command, "Front Rank, Commence," followed by the command, "Cut One."

In this practice it will be found that some positions are strong and others weak,—*i. e.* : There are some positions from which a cut can be delivered instantaneously and with great force; while others, owing to the position of the hand, cannot be made as rapidly nor with the same power. Each pupil must find out for himself which are his weak and which his strong positions, and watch closely how those he may be opposed to are effected by the same causes.

SWORD EXERCISE. 73

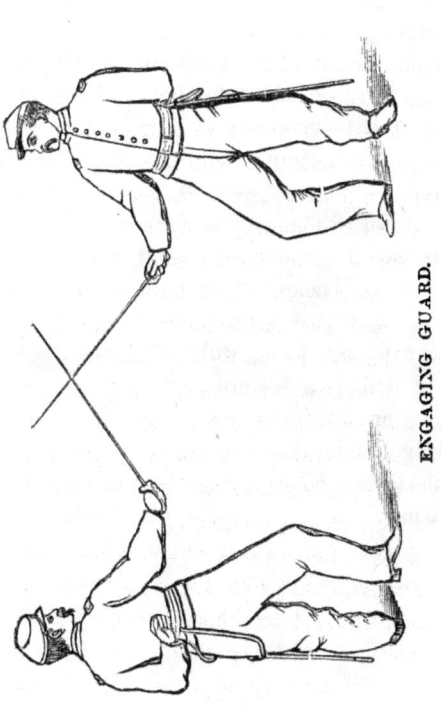

ENGAGING GUARD.

Cut One:—As soon as the order is given, the front rank will lunge out and deliver the cut; at the same time, the rear rank will spring back to the "First Position," and guard the left cheek.

The files of the rank making the cut will remain at the lunge until the next cut has been explained and the order given for its execution, when they will immediately spring up to the "First Position," and guard.

This guard will generally be found a most advantageous one for returning a cut instantly, for the reason that the back of the hand is to the front, and the arm bent in such a position that it is only necessary to extend it, with a certain degree of force, to deliver a powerful cut. When actually engaging an adversary, you must profit by this knowledge, and take care not to place him in a position where he can have the benefit of this advantage.

SWORD EXERCISE. 75

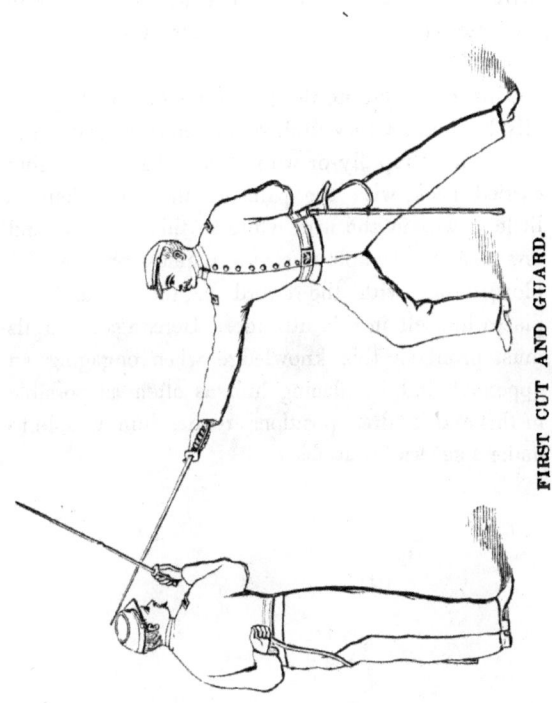

FIRST CUT AND GUARD.

Cut Two:—At the order, "Cut Two," the rear rank will lunge out to the "Third Position," and deliver the cut; the front rank will spring up to the "First Position," and make the "Second Guard."

This guard, unlike the preceding one, will generally be found a very unfavorable one for delivering a cut, either rapidly or with force. The hand being carried back, with the palm to the front, there is little power in the arm while in this position, and few men will be able to strike a quick or powerful blow, either with the sword or the hand, if he places himself in this attitude. Here, again, pupils must profit by this knowledge when engaging an opponent, and, by placing him as often as possible in this and kindred positions, render him unable to make a successful attack.

SWORD EXERCISE. 77

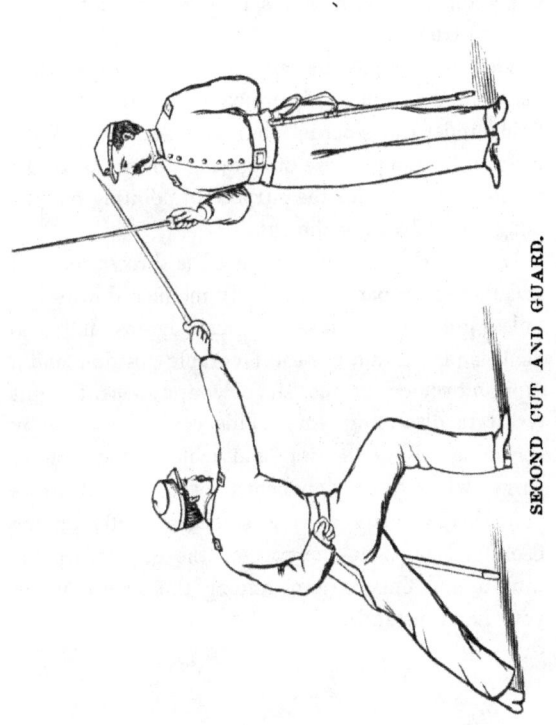

SECOND CUT AND GUARD.

7*

Cut Three:—As soon as the order is given, the front rank will lunge out and cut for the sword-arm; the rear rank will spring up and make the "Third Guard."

This is a dangerous cut to make, except when made in the manner described under the head of "Cut under the Guard;" but it is necessary to lay it down for the purpose of showing how to make the guard; and, also, for the purpose of pointing out the danger of delivering the cut.

In delivering this cut, the head is thrown forward and the upper part of the body inclines downward, unless great care be taken to guard against it. The hand is placed in a most unfavorable position, and a rapid movement on the part of your opponent might result in disarming you. This could be done by springing out of the way and making the circular parry, when your opponent's sword would strike your blade partly on the side and partly on the back, and opposite the part of the grip where the thumb and fingers join, forcing the sword out of your hand instantly.

SWORD EXERCISE. 79

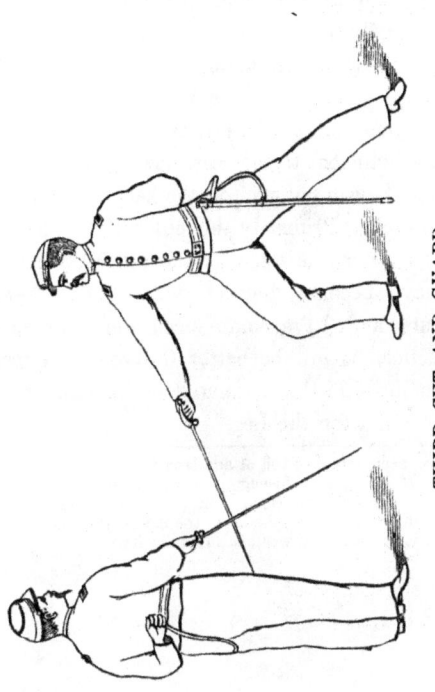

THIRD CUT AND GUARD.

Cut Four:—The rear rank will turn the hand, nails down, lunge out, and cut for the outside of the leg; the front rank will spring up and make the "Fourth Guard."

The same rule applies to this cut that does to the third cut, except that you are not liable to be disarmed* in making it. If, however, your opponent carries his right foot to the rear, out of the reach of your blade, he can cut you on the head without any risk to himself. Primarily this cut will be made in the regular order, the same as the others, but after pupils have become familiar with the different movements, and have commenced the "Independent Practice," it will be better to avoid it, except when it is made in the manner described under the head of "Feint for the Leg."

---

* It is not necessary to dwell at any length on the principles of disarming. If you oppose the edge of your sword to that of your opponent, you cannot be disarmed; but if you allow him to strike your blade on the side or on the back, the merest tyro can knock the sword out of your hand without any difficulty.

SWORD EXERCISE.

FOURTH CUT AND GUARD.

Cut Five:—The front rank will turn the hand, lunge out and cut, with the nails up; the rear rank will spring up and make the "Fifth Guard."

This guard is one of the most favorable positions in the exercise for returning an opponent's cut. By simply turning the hand you can cut seven with great force and rapidity, while your opponent, being at the lunge, will find it exceedingly difficult to get back to the guard in time to save himself. In the "Independent Practice," or when engaging an adversary, you will be careful to place your opponent in this position as rarely as possible, while you will watch your opportunity, should he place you in the position, to return his cut instantly.

SWORD EXERCISE. 83

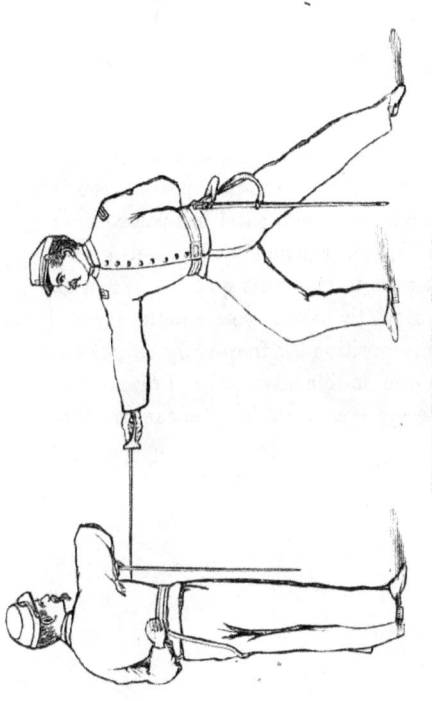

FIFTH CUT AND GUARD.

Cut Six:—The rear rank will disengage the sword, by carrying it to the rear until it clears the point of the opposing blade; they will then lunge out and cut, with the nails down. The front rank will spring up, lower the point of the sword, and make the "Sixth Guard."

This guard is much more unfavorable for returning your opponent's cut than the one just preceding it. The arm is in a cramped position, and no cut can be made until the hand has passed over a considerable space, causing delay and giving your opponent time to make his guard. When engaging an adversary, therefore, you should try and place him in this position as frequently as possible, as it will have the double advantage of discouraging him and rendering your own position comparatively safe.

SWORD EXERCISE. 85

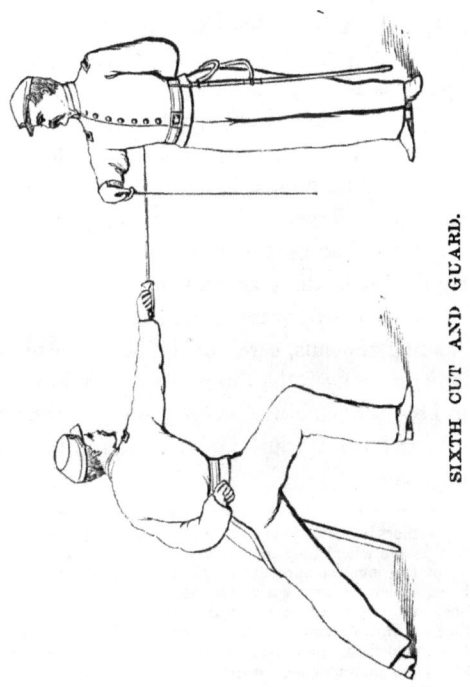

SIXTH CUT AND GUARD.

Cut Seven:—The front rank will sweep the sword across to the left, lunge out at the same time, and cut vertically down for the head. The rear rank will spring up and make the "Seventh Guard."

It will be observed that the front rank, having commenced at No. 1, continues with odd numbers, while the rear rank cuts 2, 4, and 6. In order to give both ranks an opportunity to make all the cuts, as soon as the front rank has made the "Seventh Cut," the order, "Reversed—Rear Rank Commence," will be given. The cuts will then be called off in their regular order, the rear rank making cuts 1, 3, 5, and 7, while the front rank will cut 2, 4, and 6.

In making the cuts, care should be taken to extend the arm, to keep the thumb on the back of the grip, to keep the hand well in front of the centre of the body, and to fix your eyes* steadily on those of your opponent.

---

* Many authors lay down the rule that pupils shall "glance" at the part of the person where they intend to direct a cut or point. The absurdity of this must be apparent to the merest tyro. To do this would be equivalent to giving a verbal notification to guard a certain place, and would be utterly opposed to the vital principle underlying the entire practice. The great aim of those who desire to excel as swordsmen should be to so far disconnect the hand from the eye that the muscular movement of the one will have no perceptible effect on the other. This can only be acquired by long practice; and so great is the advantage to be derived from it, that when swordsmanship was at its zenith, and the first gentlemen in the world staked their lives on the skill and dexterity with which they could wield their swords, it was deemed the very acme of the art to be able to deliver a "pass" without any movement of the eye.

SWORD EXERCISE. 87

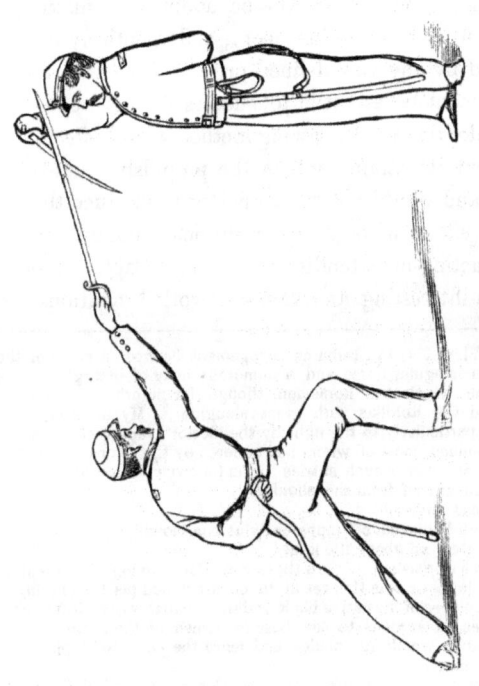

SEVENTH CUT AND GUARD.

Observations on Different Methods of Cutting.

It is a favorite theory with many authors that a "sawing" motion should be adopted in making a cut, but this is a mere theory, and is entirely unsupported by any well-defined principle. If celerity of movement be essential to success in sword exercise, the adoption of the sawing method would effectually prevent its attainment, as the propulsive action of the hand would not be sufficient to produce the desired effect without an additional motion—either contracting or extending the arm. Captain Nolan, in his interesting and valuable work,* mentions cer-

---

* " When I was in India an engagement between a party of the Nizam's irregular horse and a numerous body of insurgents took place, in which the horsemen, though far inferior in numbers, defeated the Rohillas with great slaughter. My attention was drawn particularly to the fight by the doctor's report of the killed and wounded, most of whom had suffered by the sword, and in the column of remarks such entries as the following were numerous:

"' Arm cut off from the shoulder.'

"' Head severed.'

"' Both hands cut off (apparently at one blow).'

"' Leg cut off above the knee.'

" I was astonished. Were these men giants, to lop off limbs thus wholesale ? Or was this result to be attributed (as I was told) to the sharp edge of the native blade and the peculiar way of drawing it ?

" I became anxious to see these horsemen of the Nizam, to examine their wonderful blades and learn the knack of lopping off men's limbs.

" Opportunity soon offered, for the Commander-in-Chief went to Hyderabad on a tour of inspection, on which I accompanied him. After passing the Kistna River, a squadron of these very horsemen joined the camp as part of the escort. And now fancy my astonishm nt! The sword-blades they had were chiefly old dragoon blad s c st from our service. * * * * * * * * * * *

tain facts, which came under his personal observation, that are far more important in their bearing on this subject than the most elaborate theories.

It is evident that Captain Nolan had received the impression that the terrible execution of the native horsemen was to be ascribed to a peculiar mode of drawing the sword in delivering the cut; but it did not require the statement of the Nizam's trooper to convince me that the captain was mistaken. The secret of their success, if, indeed, it may be called a secret, consists in the fact that, by the constant use of Indian clubs, and constant practice with their swords, they are perfect models of muscular development, and, their swords being ground to a fine edge, they find it an easy matter to produce effects that startle and amaze those who look only at these effects without tracing them to their legitimate causes.

Colonel Marey, of the French Army, has made many interesting experiments to show the effect produced by delivering a cut or a thrust in a certain manner, and claims to have satisfactorily demon-

---

"An old trooper of the Nizam's told me the old broad English blades were in great favor with them. * * * * "I said, 'How do you strike with your sword to cut off men's limbs?'

"'Strike hard, sir!' said the old trooper.

"'Yes, of course; but how do you teach them to use their swords in that particular way?' (drawing it.)

"'We never teach them any way, sir.'"

—" *Cavalry, its History and Tactics,*" by Capt. L. E. Nolan.

strated that the "sawing" motion is the most advantageous mode of cutting. No one can read his work* without being impressed with the skill and ability that he brings to the discussion of the subject, and the learning and research that is evinced in every page. His experiments were very extensive and his deductions generally correct; but in two instances, I am convinced that he is in error. He says the thumb should not be kept extended along the back of the grip in cutting; and that the "sawing" motion should be observed. By conforming to the first rule a man would lose much of the control over his sword which it is essential to possess; while, by observing the second, he would neutralize the effect to be obtained from the velocity of the sword at the moment of impact. But the advocates of the sawing movement overlook one important feature of the subject. They appear to forget that to attempt to deliver a cut that would be sufficient to take off a man's head or his limbs before he had been partially disabled by a less powerful blow, would be a piece of folly that no practical swordsman would be guilty of. Light, close, rapid cuts are always preferable if you are opposed to a good swordsman. They are more likely to reach him than a more powerful cut that would require more time

---

* "Mémoire sur les Armes-blanches."

in its delivery and would carry the hand over a wider space, thus giving your opponent notice of your intended movement and leaving yourself open to his attack. If light, quick cuts fail to take off heads or limbs, they are always the safest, and will disconcert if they do not disable an opponent; that done, the result is inevitable.

Points and Parries.

After the introduction of gunpowder for war purposes, the two-handed swords that had been rendered necessary by the heavy armor of the fifteenth and sixteenth centuries, were discarded, and the knights and soldiers of that period took a wild plunge from the ponderous blades, in wielding which they required all the strength of both hands, to the light, taper rapier, requiring scarcely more than the touch of the thumb and first finger.

The first book on fencing was published in Italy in 1536, and the Italians cultivated fencing very assiduously, and sent teachers of the art into Spain and other countries; but the rapier was not introduced into England until 1571.

An indefinite number of points may be made on the same principle that an indefinite number of cuts can be made; but, for all practical purposes, it will be found that three "parries" or movements of the blade in different directions will be sufficient to throw off the point of either sword, bayonet or lance, no matter from what direction it may be aimed.

In the ancient Italian school there were eight parries, designated by the Italian numerals, "primo," "secondo," "terzo," "quarto," &c., and from these were derived the modern terms with which fencing-masters delight to puzzle the brains of their pupils. There can be no excuse at the present day and in an English-speaking community for adhering to these terms when their English equivalents would answer the purpose better.

With the small sword, or foil, the terms "quarte" (carte) and "tierce" were used in a general sense to indicate that the nails were up or down, and all the points were made from one of these positions. But with the broad sword, the short sword, or the musket and bayonet, these terms are worthless, for the reason that they fail to describe the position of the hand—as it frequently happens that the nails are neither up nor down.

Observations on Thrusting.

The practical utility of thrusting with the sword is open to grave doubts; while in several well-authenticated cases, this mode of attack has resulted most disastrously to the persons employing it.

Kinglake, in his History of the War in the Crimea, cites two instances where officers came near losing their lives in consequence of their swords becoming fast in the bodies of their antagonists, and their consequent inability to defend themselves against the attack of another enemy in their immediate vicinity. This could never have occurred if the edge of the sword had been used instead of the point; for no matter what the effect of the cut might be, the sword would still be free, and could be used instantly for either offensive or defensive purposes.

At the battle of Balaklava, Captain Morris,* who

---

* "It so happened that Capt. Morris, the officer in command of the 17th Lancers, was advancing in front of his left squadron, and thence it resulted that the portion of the regiment which outflanked the battery fell under his personal leadership * * * * *
In the direct front of the ranks, thus awaiting the charge of our horsemen, there was sitting in his saddle a Russian who seemed to be the squadron-leader. Morris drove his horse full at this officer, and in the instant which followed the contact, the sword of the assailant had transfixed the trunk of the Russian, passing through with such force that its hilt pressed against the man's body.   *   *   *   *   *   *   *   *   *   *
For a moment there was nothing to hinder the enemy from capturing any of the English who here remained wounded and disabled. Of these Morris himself was one; and his misfortune was a consequence of the determination which induced him to 'give point' to his adversary. 'I don't know,' he would afterwards say, 'I don't know how I came to use the *point* of my sword, but it is the last time I ever do.'

"When his sword, driving home to the hilt, ran through the Russian squadron-leader whom he had singled out for his first adversary, the Russian tumbled over on the off-side of his horse, drawing down with him in his fall the sword which had slain him; and since Morris, with all his strength, was unable to withdraw the blade, and yet did not choose to let go his grasp of the handle, or to disengage himself from the wrist-knot, it resulted that, though commanded the Seventeenth Lancers, rode into the Russian ranks at the head of his men; and, having singled out the Russian squadron-leader, he ran him through the body; but being unable to extricate his sword in time to defend himself, he was cut down by a Russian dragoon.

On the same day, when the "Heavy Brigade" charged the Russian cavalry, Lieutenant Eliott,* an officer on the staff of General Scarlett, attacked a Russian officer, and delivered a thrust, driving his sword to the hilt in the body of his adversary; but before he could withdraw his blade he was carried forward into the ranks of the enemy.

---

still in his saddle, he was tethered to the ground by his own sword-arm.

"Whilst thus disabled, Morris received a sabre-cut on the left side of the head, which carried away a large piece of bone above the ear, and a deep, clean cut passing down through the acorn of his forage-cap, which penetrated both plates of the skull."

* "The Brigadier now found himself nearing the front of the column at a point very near its centre, and the spot at which Scarlett thus rode was marked by the presence of a Russian officer who sat erect in his saddle some few paces in front of his people, and confronting the English intruder * * * * * *
Moved perhaps by such indication of rank as was to be gathered in one fleeting moment from the sight of a staff-officer's hat, the Russian officer chose Eliott for his adversary, * * *
he faced him as he approached, and endeavored to cut him down. Evading or parrying the cut, Eliott drove his sword through the body of his assailant, and the swiftness with which he was galloping up, whilst delivering this thrust, was so great that the blade darted in to the very hilt; but until the next moment, when Eliott's charger had rushed past, the weapon, though held fast by its owner, still could not be withdrawn. Thence it resulted that the Russian officer was turned round in his saddle by the leverage of the sword which transfixed him."—*The Invasion of the Crimea*, by A. W. Kinglake.

This result may be partly attributed to the momentum which the forward movement of the horse lent to the sword at the instant the point was delivered; but the same disaster might have befallen an officer on foot, and engaged in a mêlée, while it is scarcely possible that it could occur if an officer relied upon the edge and not upon the point of his sword. The case of General Scarlett*, on the occasion when Captain Morris and Lieutenant Eliott came near losing their lives, is a remarkable illustration of the correctness of this view, and it is further confirmed by another incident at the same battle. Sergeant-Major John Grieve, of the Second Dragoons, went to the rescue of an officer who was wounded and surrounded by Russian cavalry. Dashing in

---

* "It was by digging his charger right in between the two nearest troopers before him that Scarlett wedged himself into the solid mass of the enemy's squadrons. * * * Scarlett observed that of the adversaries nearest to him, whom he had not, he knew, gravely wounded, there were some who dropped off their horses without having been killed or wounded by him; and it seemed to him, if he were to judge only from his own eyes, that they were throwing themselves to the ground of their own accord. * * * * * * * *

From the moment when the Brigadier had thus established himself in the midst of his foes, it resulted, of course, that his tenure of life was by the sword, and not by the sword which is a metaphor, but by that which is actual, and of steel. Scarlett, it seems, had no pretension to be more than a passably good swordsman, and he had the disadvantage of being near-sighted; but he knew how to handle his weapon, and in circumstances which exposed him to an attack from several at the same time, he had more need of such unflagging industry of the sword-arm as might keep the blade flashing here, there, and all sides, in quickly successive whirls, than of the subtle, the delicate skill which prepares men for combats of two."—*Kinglake's Crimea.*

among the latter he swept his sword round to the right and left, cutting off the head of one, wounding others, and scattering the remainder so as to enable the officer, whose life he had saved, to ride away without further injury. For his gallant conduct on this occasion, he received the Victoria Cross.

Distinct from the proofs contained in the incidents described, history teaches that amongst the nations and tribes which have become most famous for their swords, and the manner in which they use them, the straight sword or sword used for thrusting, is entirely unknown. At the battle of the Pyramids, the Mamelukes, armed with light, curved sabres, swept down with resistless fury on the French infantry, and actually rode into and over their squares. In the various wars between Turkey and Russia, the Turkish and Circassian cavalry, armed with scimitars and yataghans, committed such havoc among the Russians that the ponderous cuirassiers were wont to seek shelter, from the terrible blades of their foes, behind squares of infantry and masses of artillery. During the war on the Punjaub, the Sikh horsemen not only met the English cavalry hand-to-hand, but individual soldiers challenged English dragoons to meet them in single combat. In one of these encounters, at Chillianwalla, a Sikh cut down and unhorsed three English dragoons in succession, and would doubtless have committed more damage had he not been *shot* down. The history of the same battle furnishes another striking illustration of the relative value of the point and edge of the sword.

A dragoon of the Third Regiment, charging with his squadron, made a thrust at the Sikh next him; the sword *stuck* in the lower part of his body, but did not penetrate sufficiently to disable him, when the Sikh *cut* back, hit the dragoon across the mouth, and took his head clean off.

And the French cavalry, when it had reached its highest point in efficiency and fame, and was led by the most dauntless and brilliant soldiers that the country had ever produced, relied mainly on the edge of the sword; although the use of the small sword was cultivated more in France than in any other nation at the period referred to.

I have deemed it proper to dwell at some length upon this branch of the subject, and to cite those practical examples of the effect of adopting a false theory, for the purpose of correcting a pernicious practice that has crept into existence through the employment of mere fencing-masters (who are not soldiers) to teach the use of the sword, and by the substitution of the foil for the sword (or its counterpart) in practising.

While fencing may be justly regarded as a healthy and elegant exercise, for *civilians*, the use of the foil is calculated to engender the most erroneous impressions on the minds of officers, who may be called upon at any time to defend their lives with their swords. The flexibility of the foil will enable an expert fencer to produce effects that may dazzle the uninitiated, while they are well understood, and known to be mere sleight-of-hand tricks by those familiar with the exercise. If an expert fencer makes a rapid pass over his opponent's guard, striking his foil near its centre, with force, against that of his opponent, he can spring the point of his foil from ten to eighteen inches, according to the flexibility of his blade; whereas if he makes a cut with a sword, using equal force and striking with the edge of his blade, he can not spring the point of his weapon the hundredth part of an inch. Any one desiring to test these characteristics of the sword and the foil, can do so by placing a board, of six or eight inches in width, on its edge upon a table; and, after making an eight or ten pound weight fast with a short string to the button of the foil, and placing the foil, a third of its length from the hilt, across the edge of the board, while one hand is kept on the hilt and the other raises the weight, so as to allow the point of the blade to get the proper elevation, and then by letting go the weight and allowing it to carry the point with it, while one hand remains on the hilt, it will be found that the foil will bend until the table checks the downward course of the weight. But if a sword be placed, *on its edge*, in the same position, and the weight be doubled or quadrupled, it will be found that the point of the blade will not be changed a single degree by the weight suspended from it. Nor is this the only objection to the foil. If a foil be curved, the object is to heighten the effect of the pass already described; and, in making the pass, the concave side leads—while in making a similar pass with a sword the convex surface of the blade would lead. Added to this, the rectangular form of the blade leaves the mind in doubt as to the position of the hand when using a sword; as, in the one case, you may oppose any side of the blade to your opponent, while in the other, the edge must invariably (except in the circular parry) be presented to the blade of your adversary.

But, however men may differ as to the propriety of thrusting with the sword, there can be no difference of opinion as to the necessity for knowing how to parry a thrust. For drill purposes, therefore, and for the purpose of affording beginners an opportunity to practise and to become familiar with the principles involved, three "points," with the corresponding "parries," will be laid down in this system. These "points" may be made either from the "engaging guard" or from any other guard that will place the hand in a position to execute them.

Points and Parries.

First Point:—The class being at the "Engaging Guard," the instructor will give the cautionary command: "Front rank commence," when the rear rank will immediately spring back to the "first position," and will bring the sword to a position nearly perpendicular, edge to the right, point inclining to the front, hand opposite the right nipple, the elbow raised, and the thumb and fingers encircling* the grip. At the command "two," the front rank will turn the hand so as to bring the edge of the sword up and the nails to the right, and will lunge out and deliver the point at the chests of the opposing rank. At the instant the movement is commenced by the front rank, the point of the sword should be directed at the faces of the opposite rank; but by raising the hand, and making the point of the sword describe an arc of a circle, the parry will be rendered more difficult.

---

* In making the circular parry the position of the hand is changed; the thumb and fingers grasp the handle, and you oppose the *back* of your sword to your opponent's blade, while at all other times the thumb is extended on the back of the grip, and the edge of your sword presented to that of your opponent.

SWORD EXERCISE. 101

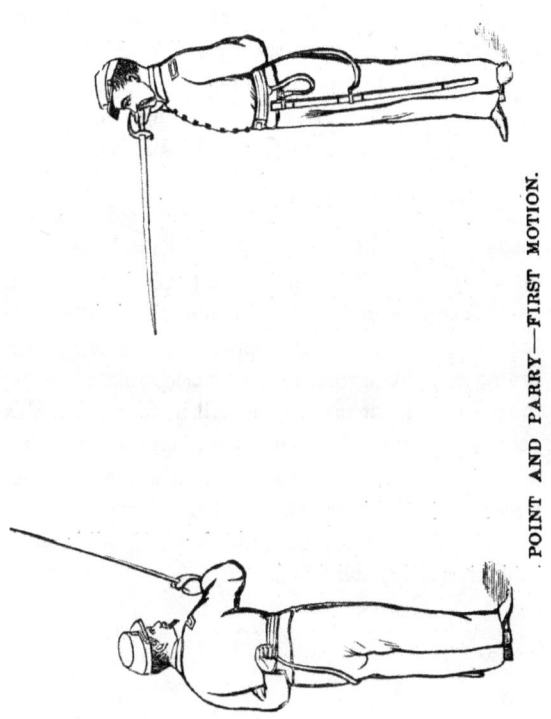

POINT AND PARRY—FIRST MOTION.

The Parry:—The rear rank will remain steady until their opponents' swords are so close that they can be "parried" with certainty. They will then make a rapid pass, with their own swords, across in front of them, the point falling over to the left—edge up—and will strike the opposing swords, with the *back of the blade*, and carry the hand to the right until it clears the right side.

This parry will serve against any point that is made slowly; and is particularly adapted to throw off a bayonet thrust, which, being given with both hands, requires more force than a sword thrust to turn it aside. But when opposed to a small sword or other light sword that is susceptible of being moved with great rapidity, it will be found that this parry is rather to be avoided than practised, and that a rapid movement of the sword in a direction opposite to that in which the hand happens to be placed, will generally be the best protection against a thrust quickly delivered.

SWORD EXERCISE. 103

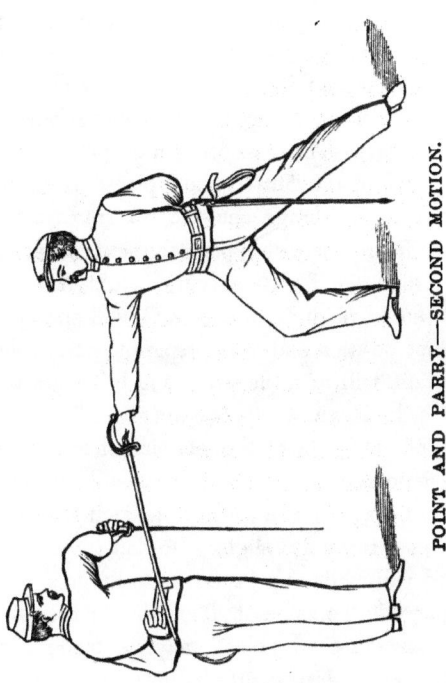

POINT AND PARRY—SECOND MOTION.

In ordinary practice the "first point" can be made from either the second or seventh guard, by merely bringing the point of the sword to the front, *with the edge up;* and lunging out from the first to the third position. This may be done to disconcert an opponent or to make an impetuous adversary keep his distance, but for other purposes it is not desirable.

Second Point:—The class being in the position that the execution of the "first point" placed them, the front rank at the lunge, and the rear rank at the parry, the instructor will explain the next movement and give the order for its execution. At the command, "second point," the front rank will spring up to the first position and will prepare to parry; and the rear rank will turn the sword and bring it across the body as high as in the "engaging guard," but with the edge of the blade to the left, and the nails up. At the command "two," the rear rank will lunge out to the third position and deliver the point; raising the hand and turning it slightly, so that the edge of the sword will incline up instead of to the left.

The parry is the same as described for the "first point." The "second point" may be made from either the first or third guards by lowering or raising the point of the sword; or from the "engaging guard," by simply turning the hand.

SWORD EXERCISE. 105

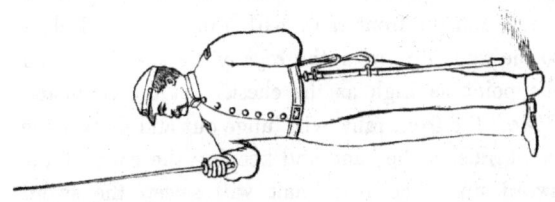

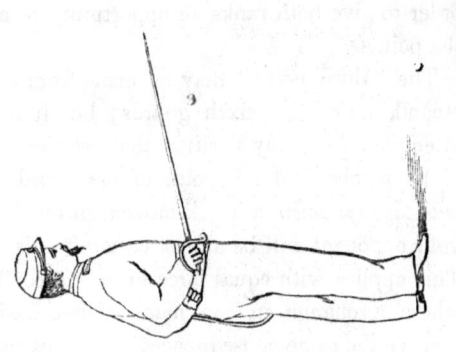

THIRD POINT.

Third Point:—The rear rank being at the lunge, the instructor will explain the next movement and will command, "third point," at the last sound of which the rear rank will spring up and prepare to parry, and the front rank will bring the hand close to the right hip, with the *edge of the sword up*, and the point as high as the chest. At the command "two," the front rank will lunge out and deliver the point, raising the hand and keeping the edge of the sword up. The rear rank will sweep the sword round to the left and make the parry.

The front rank having made the first and third points, the instructor will repeat the commands in order to give both ranks an opportunity to make all the points.

The "third point" may be made from either the second, fourth, or sixth guards; but if it is ever attempted from any position that requires the hand to be turned, and the point of the sword lowered, *with the edge down*, a quick movement on the part of your opponent will be almost certain to disarm you. This applies with equal force to the "second point," where a change in the manner described might involve the same consequences; but does not apply to a point delivered from either the "engaging guard" or the "seventh guard," provided the point of your sword be kept well raised, viz.: as high as your eyes.

Parries.

The other parries referred to are made generally by turning the hand so that the *edge of your sword* will strike your opponent's blade; when the lever power of your hand, acting on the "feeble" of your opponent's sword, will carry his point out of the line of defence. For instance: If the "second point" be made "over the guard" by your opponent, while you are at the "engaging guard," your defence is already made; provided, that at the instant he withdraws his blade from yours, you allow your sword to move slightly to the right, without turning the hand. But if the point be made "under the guard," when the edge of your sword is to the right, turn your hand and strike the "feeble" of your opponent's blade, with the "fort" of your own, and it will be immediately thrown out of the line of projection.

These rules apply to every position in which the hand may be placed; but there are certain movements which have advantages over others, for the reason that they place the hand in a more favorable position for countering on an opponent.

The Feints.

A "Feint" is a rapid movement of the sword in one direction, while the real attack is intended for the opening made by the attempt to meet the feint.

Several "Feints" may be made, but there are only two that are really effective. The most important of these is the "Feint for the Leg and Cut for the Head." The class being formed (files facing each other), the order is given, "Guard;" then the caution, "Front Rank—Commence," and the order, "Leg." The front rank will raise the hand and carry it to the right, extending the arm until the "fort" of one sword presses against the "feeble" of the opposing sword, which they will force to the right until the point is clear of the body, and then, by a rapid movement, "Feint" for the outside of the advanced legs of the rear rank; the swords should be checked, when well down towards the knee, and the "Seventh Cut" delivered.

Instead of guarding the leg, the rear rank will spring up quickly and carry the right foot six inches to the rear of the left, the toe resting lightly on the ground, and both knees straight; at the same time they will make the "Seventh Guard."

At the order, "Guard," both ranks will return to the "Engage." The caution, "Rear Rank—Commence," will be given, and the "Feint" and "Cut" will be made, by the rear rank, in the same manner.

In this combination, it is necessary to be extremely careful, (1) That the thumb be kept on the back of the grip, that the movement of the sword be very rapid, and that it be carried well up along the oppos-

SWORD EXERCISE. 109

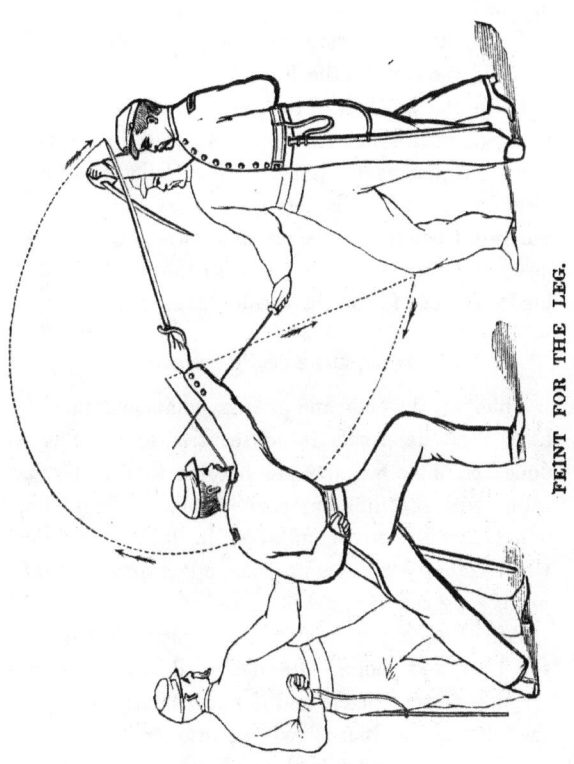

FEINT FOR THE LEG.

ing blade; and, (2) That the head be kept well up, and the eyes on those of your opponent while making the feint.

The next in importance is the "Feint for the Left side and the Cut for the Right."

Raise the hand as in the previous feint, and force your opponent's blade to the right; then, by a quick movement, clear the point of his blade with your own, and feint for his left side, breast high; check the sword before it reaches him, sweep it over his head, describing a semi-circle with the point of your blade, and cut for his right side, breast high.

Independent Practice.

Thus far, the cuts and guards, points and parries, have been described in consecutive order; this is done to enable beginners to become thoroughly familiar with the different positions and changes, but is not intended to be followed in this practice, or when actually "Engaging" an adversary. *In this practice, the cuts, &c., are not called off.*

After crossing swords at the "Engaging Guard," the cuts and points are delivered whenever an opening presents itself, and if not instantly returned, the "Engaging Guard" will be resumed.

All the knowledge that has been acquired in previous lessons may be now brought into requisition; the left foot need no longer be kept in the same place, and the "Advance" and "Retire" may be practised as occasion requires.

There must be no wild slashing, and no reckless thrusting. The swords must touch lightly, but still with the certainty that they *do* touch; and the movements must be executed with promptness, dexterity and ease. It was a favorite expression of Bartrand, a celebrated French fencing-master and teacher of the body-guard of Charles X.: "You must think and see with the ends of your fingers." If not literally true, this, at least, serves to show the importance that its author attached to preserving the touch. And when I add that Bartrand was a professor in the polytechnic school in Paris, it will be readily understood that he was no mean authority on the subject.

In addition to the cuts and thrusts already described, there are two other cuts that may be brought into requisition in this practice.

These are light, quick, close movements, and are not intended to do any serious damage; but they serve to disconcert an opponent, and to test his skill in the more subtle branches of the art.

The first of these is the "cut over the guard." This is made by advancing the hand until the "fort" of one sword presses against the "feeble" of the other; the hand is then carried rapidly to the right, then raised, and with a quick, forward movement, the cut is made for the upper part of the wrist.

112 SWORD EXERCISE.

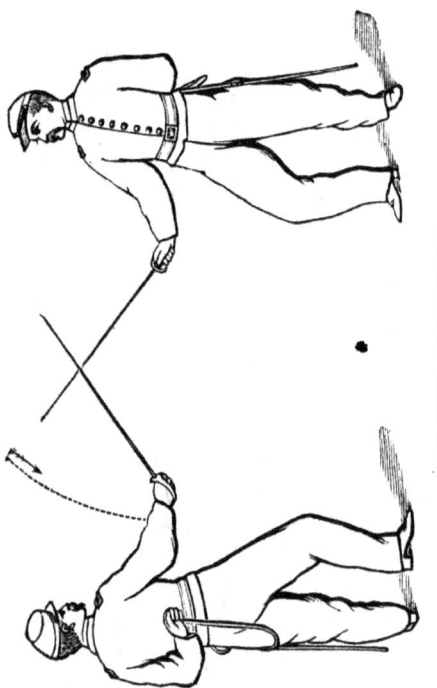

CUT OVER THE GUARD

To "Guard," keep a steady pressure against the opposing blade, which has to be withdrawn before the cut can be made; or "disengage" by dropping your point and returning to the "engaging guard."

Cut Under the Guard:—This is a dangerous and very annoying cut to any one not familiar with the proper defence; but care must be taken in making it to carry the opposing sword well to your right, as a failure to do this, and a rapid extension of your opponent's arm, might involve serious consequences. By running the hilt of your own sword up to within a few inches of the point of your opponent's blade, you can force his blade across with ease, when his sword-arm from the wrist to the elbow will be exposed.

Raise the hand (as in the "cut over the guard") until the point of the opposing sword has been carried well to the right; then sweep your blade rapidly to the rear, describing a circle with the point, and cut up for your opponent's wrist; spring back to the "engaging guard."

The guard is made by springing up to the first position and turning the hand, so as to bring the edge of the sword to the left with the point down— essentially the same as the "third guard."

114   SWORD EXERCISE.

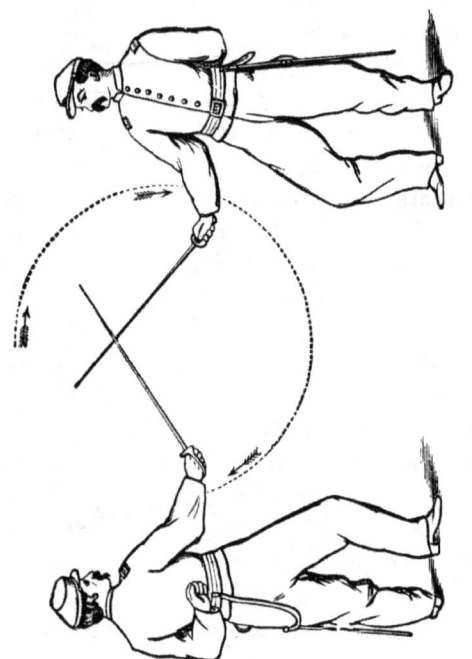

CUT UNDER THE GUARD.

SWORD EXERCISE. 115

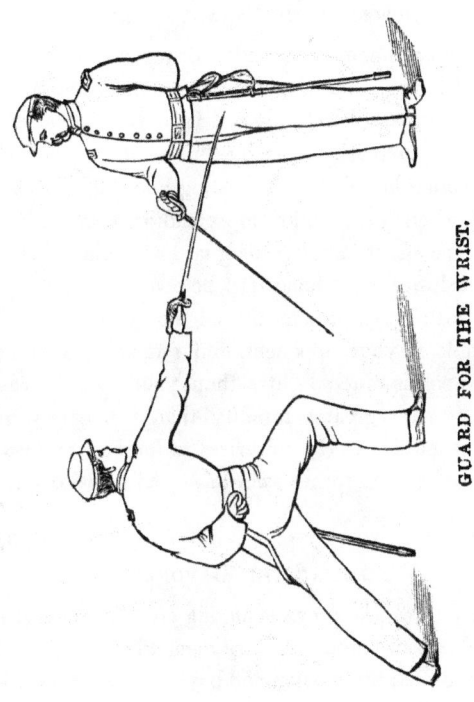

GUARD FOR THE WRIST.

The two cuts last described will be found of great importance in

Opposing the Small-sword.

As your opponent, in endeavoring to reach your *body* with the *point* of his weapon must necessarily expose his *sword-arm;* do not imitate his example by trying to reach his body, but content yourself with feeling his blade and cutting under or over his guard when he attempts to extend his arm. If he should persist in making his guard with his nails up, raise or lower your hand if it be necessary to disengage, but always present the edge of your sword to the blade of your opponent, and remember that, as his weapon is much lighter than your own, he can move it with greater rapidity than you can your weapon, but is utterly powerless so long as you confine your attack to his sword-arm, and make only light, rapid passes.

Opposing the Bayonet.

An impression prevails among civilians, and to a limited extent among military men, who are not well informed, that the musket and bayonet has the advantage over the sword in single combat. This impression is entirely erroneous, and is unsustained by any well-defined scientific principle, or any practical test that can entitle it to a moment's consideration. On the contrary, there are thousands of well-authenticated cases on record where men who were not expert swordsmen have defeated men of equal or superior strength, armed with muskets and bayonets. The lance may be considered a formidable weapon under certain circumstances, but in a mêlée, or a hand-to-hand fight, when opposed to the sword, it is utterly worthless. The same may be said of the bayonet. The weight of the piece renders it unwieldy; while the leverage is so great, when the arms are extended, that the blow of an ordinary cane is sufficient to throw it out of the line of projection. Added to this, both hands are exposed to the edge of the sword, a circumstance that is sure to engender a feeling of constraint, if not of fear, in the mind of any man who finds himself thus opposed to a good swordsman. When opposed to the small-sword, the aim should be to keep out of the reach of your opponent; but when opposed to the bayonet, the aim should be to keep as close to him as possible. Hence, the moment you find yourself opposed to a man with a musket and bayonet, you should gain ground upon him, keeping your sword in front of you at the "engaging guard," and raising or lowering your hand to correspond with any elevation or depression of his bayonet. If he stands on the defensive, make two or three rapid feints and force him to place his piece in a position that will enable you to strike his hands or head, or, tempt him to lunge. This is his weakest position. Test it on drill by placing a strong man at the lunge, with his arms fully extended, and take the point of his bayonet between your thumb and first finger; when you will find that you can force it to the right or left with ease, and the most powerful man you can select will be unable to retain his piece in this position if the slightest pressure is brought to bear upon it. It follows, therefore, that if you can induce your adversary to lunge, you have him at your mercy. The circular parry, or a movement analogous to that, will place the hand in the most favorable position for delivering an effective cut; but any movement of the sword that will force the bayonet out of the direct line, combined with a quick spring forward and a rapid sweep of the sword along the musket or across the arms or face of your opponent, will render the struggle of short duration. Few men can wield a musket and bayonet with one hand—none can do it effectively. Both hands are exposed; and if one of them can be rendered useless, the bravest man will be unable to defend himself successfully.

General Observations.

No work that can be written will enable you to become a good swordsman, unless you grapple with the details of the subject and analyze its subtle intricacies for yourself. No author, however conscientious, will tell all that he knows, and no instructor, however efficient, will teach all that *he* knows. It may seem paradoxical, to say that the most elaborate work would contain too little, while the most meagre treatise would be pretty sure to contain too much.

In the preceding pages, much is laid down that may be deemed unnecessary by those who are disposed to be captious, and something may have been omitted that they would deem of importance; but those who are sincerely desirous of obtaining information that will enable them to form a tolerably correct estimate of the importance of knowing how to use their arms, and of the relative value of different systems, may find some useful suggestions that have not been borrowed from other authors, and some deductions that are drawn from a pretty thorough investigation of the subject after several years of assiduous practice.

I have already reverted to the fact, that some of the guards prescribed will be found weak and some strong. No absolute rule can be laid down; but it will generally be found that the first, fifth and seventh guards are the most favorable positions in which the hand can be placed for instantly returning your opponent's cut. A rapid and powerful cut can be made from the first guard, by simply extending the arm. A tremendous cut may be delivered from the fifth guard by simply turning the hand; but the most formidable of all is the cut from the seventh guard, when your opponent's sword-arm is extended, and his left side, from temple to hip, is exposed and within your reach. To render any of these cuts effective they must be delivered with the rapidity of lightning, the instant your opponent's blade touches yours. If he cuts seven, the proximity of his blade to your head may make you apprehensive of danger, but there is none. The force of the cut is spent the moment his sword strikes yours, and it would be necessary, in order to do you any damage, for him to raise his sword again before he could strike you on the head. This he will have no time to do, as your sword must inevitably reach him before he can complete the motion of raising his blade.

In practising, gentlemen should remember that they are not supposed to injure each other; and when a class is being instructed, the instructor should change the position of the pupils, not allowing the same persons to oppose each other at two successive lessons; and should insist, kindly but firmly, on the observance between pupils of the courteous manners and gentlemanly deportment which should always characterize officers in their intercourse with each other.

www.ingramcontent.com/pod-product-compliance
Lightning Source LLC
Chambersburg PA
CBHW070202100426
42743CB00013B/3020